wholesome meals for

babies
and
toddlers

healthy food your kids will love to eat

wholesome meals for

babies
and
toddlers

healthy food your kids will love to eat

p

This is a Parragon Publishing Book
First published in 2006

Parragon Publishing
Queen Street House
4 Queen Street
Bath BA1 1HE, UK

ISBN: 1-40546-845-9
Printed in Indonesia

Produced by The Bridgewater Book Company Ltd
Photographer: Clive Bozzard-Hill
Home economist: Sandra Baddeley

Notes for the Reader
This book uses imperial, metric, or US cup measurements.
Follow the same units of measurement throughout; do not mix
imperial and metric. All spoon measurements are level: teaspoons
are assumed to be 5 ml, and tablespoons are assumed to be 15 ml.
Unless breast or formula milk is stated, milk is assumed to be whole,
eggs and individual vegetables such as potatoes are medium, and
pepper is freshly ground black pepper. Recipes using raw or very
lightly cooked eggs should be avoided by infants, the elderly, pregnant
women, convalescents, and anyone suffering from an illness. Whole
nuts and seeds are not recommended for children under five years
of age. Nut butters and very finely chopped or crushed nuts and seeds
are fine for babies of 1 year or older, unless there has been a history of
allergies to nuts or seeds within the family. If you have any concerns,
please discuss it with your health practitioner.

Picture acknowledgments
The Bridgewater Book Company would like to thank the following for
permission to reproduce copyright material:
Michael Keller/Corbis page 6; Taxi/Getty Images page 10;
Don Mason/Corbis page 13; Ariel Skelley/Corbis pages 14 and 38;
Edward Bock/Corbis page 20; Altrendo/Getty Images page 22;
Dex Images, Inc./Corbis page 26; Gareth Brown/Corbis page 50;
Larry Williams/Corbis front cover (bottom centre) and page 62;
Phototonica/Getty Images page 76 and Gerhard Steiner/Corbis page 94.

Contents

introduction

Having a baby is a bit like being on a roller coaster: no sooner have you mastered (or at least become accustomed to) breast- or bottle-feeding than it's time to tackle a new stage in your baby's development—many parents feel distinctly nervous about the prospect of introducing solids to their child's diet but, take a deep breath, it really is quite straightforward.

What to feed and when are the two main concerns of parents. Up until quite recently it was usual for parents to begin weaning at four months. Now, many more recent studies have concluded that there is no nutritional benefit in introducing solids before a baby is six months old and that breast-feeding is the best form of nutrition for babies up until this age. Many quite ordinary foods can cause allergies, and most babies' digestive systems are unable to cope with anything more than breast or formula milk before six months.

For parents who feel that their baby is ready for solids, the first purées you give should be regarded as simply a taster of what's to come and as a supplement to breast or formula milk. Only introduce solids when your baby can sit up and has begun to exercise some control over his or her tongue.

The aim of this book is to ease any anxieties you may have about weaning and to smooth the path from your baby's first taste of solids to his or her participation in family meals. The advice is designed to be practical and reassuring, to help you give your baby the best start in life. Many parents feel that they don't have the required time or skills to prepare homemade baby foods, but they couldn't be easier to make and, especially if prepared in bulk, involve minimal time. By making your own foods, you can also familiarize your baby with a wide range of tastes and textures.

Every baby and toddler is different, with his or her own particular likes and dislikes, which can sometimes change on a daily basis. For example, some children may initially adore a particular food to the extent that they can't eat enough of it, only to reject it the next time they are offered it. Most parents will vouch that this behavior is common. However perturbed or frustrated you may feel, it is counterproductive to force your baby to eat and can lead to mealtimes becoming a form of power game. Many parents recall times when their child ate nothing but toast for weeks without any adverse effects, which is reassuring to us all.

Is your baby ready?

Your baby is ready to take his or her first spoonful from six months. Experts agree that a baby's digestive system is too immature for solids before this age, and early weaning can put stress on the kidneys, as well as trigger possible allergies. Breast or formula milk provides all the nutrients a baby needs for the first six months.

All babies are different and progress at their own pace, but the following may indicate that your baby is ready for solids:

▸ has gained significant weight and can hold head up and sit comfortably in a highchair

▸ can close mouth around spoon, and can move tongue back and forth while holding food in

▸ starts demanding more frequent feeds

▸ shows an interest in your food

Weaning guidelines

Although most foods are now thought to be suitable from six months (see page 27 for the exceptions), it's advisable to take the process of weaning slowly, so start with baby rice or a few simple fruit or vegetable purées and progress to combinations of puréed food, with or without cereals, in the first few weeks. Remember that milk—breast and formula—is still an important part of a baby's diet.

▸ Don't force-feed your baby: eating is a new skill, which should be accomplished gradually. Your baby is exercising previously unused muscles and will initially try to suck food, which explains why it is often pushed out of the mouth or appears to be "spat" out.

▸ Be scrupulous about hygiene: make sure that all spoons and bowls are sterilized and don't store any leftover food for later use, because it could be a breeding ground for bacteria. Give your baby his or her own eating utensils.

▸ Choose the right time to introduce solids: it's important to pick a time when you're not feeling rushed and your baby is not too tired or hungry—the middle of the day is often seen as the best option. It may be a good idea to give your baby a little milk first to curb any hunger pangs, but as feeding becomes established, start to offer food before milk.

▸ Face-to-face interaction is important: try to be as encouraging as possible by smiling and offering lots of praise—even if your baby manages only a spoonful at first.

First foods

To begin with, offer a little baby rice or a fruit or vegetable purée (see pages 28–37) on the tip of a shallow plastic spoon or your finger. Commercial baby rice is readily available, but it is also simple and quick to prepare your own (see page 28), and then freeze in convenient-sized portions. Don't expect your baby to eat more than a tablespoon or even less—at this stage, the amount that is eaten by your child is immaterial.

For the first few weeks, offer the same food for around three days at a time to enable your baby to get used to new tastes and for you to gauge if there is any form of allergic reaction. Thin and runny single-ingredient purées made from fairly mild-tasting fruit and vegetables, such as potatoes, well-cooked carrots, apples, pears, and bananas, are generally best. Wash the fruit or vegetables thoroughly and peel them, removing any core or seeds. At the next stage, and if your baby is happily accepting the food that you are offering, you can start to increase the number of solid feeds from one to two, then progress to three a day. Water or non-citrus diluted fruit juice can now replace the lunchtime milk or formula feed. Again, introduce new foods gradually and, if a new food is rejected, don't try it again for a few days or, alternatively, combine it with baby rice or another type of purée.

Early weaning

Early weaning can occur after 4 months in some cases. Be aware of the following foods up to the age of 36 months:

Age 4–12 months:
Avoid citrus fruit and juices, egg whites, nuts, nut butters, seeds, berries, fish, shellfish, chilies, corn, soy, chocolate, honey, cow's milk, goat's milk, sheep's milk, sugar, salt, soft cheese, bleu cheese, and small, hard foods. You can introduce wheat-based cereals, breads, some dairy products, and puréed or finely ground meat and poultry at 6-9 months old.

Age 12–36 months:
Avoid introducing low-fat milk before the age of 24 months, and be aware of allergens such as fish, shellfood, and nuts through to 36 months.

What do babies need?

While the saying "you are what you eat" may be an overused cliché, it's not far from the truth. Health experts now suggest that what we eat in childhood has implications for our future health. Consequently, it's crucial for parents to encourage their child to enjoy a varied diet as soon as possible.

Milk

For the first six months of your baby's life, breast or formula milk provides all the nutrients and nourishment he or she needs for growth and development. Breast or formula milk should form a major part of your baby's life up until a year old, when whole cow's milk can be introduced as a drink.

Experts firmly believe that breast milk is best for a baby, since it provides the correct balance of vitamins, minerals, and fats in a readily digestible form. Breast milk contains the antibodies necessary to help fight off infections, and research shows that it may also improve mental development in the long term. At some stage you may wish to introduce a bottle for at least some of the milk feeds if, for instance, you are returning to work. This transition will take time, so be patient with yourself and your baby.

Breads and cereals

Breads and cereals, which are also called starchy foods, are an excellent source of energy, vitamins, minerals, and fiber. Bread, pasta, potatoes, rice, and low-sugar breakfast cereals should form a major part of the diet. Two to three servings are recommended each day after the first six to eight months.

Fruit and vegetables

Fresh, frozen, and canned fruit and vegetables are an essential part of a baby's diet. They are perfect first foods, providing rich sources of vitamins, minerals, and fiber. From six months, provide a variety of fresh produce to your baby, building up to at least five different types of fruit or vegetables a day, cut up pea-sized, soft-cooked or cut up raw and shredded.

Meat, poultry, egg yolks, and vegetarian alternatives

These are a good source of protein, essential for growth and repair. Your child should be given a protein food every day after weaning; this may include vegetarian alternatives such as beans and lentils. Egg yolks should be well cooked.

Dairy foods

Milk, cheese, and yogurt provide protein, vitamins, and minerals, particularly calcium, for healthy bones and teeth. Cow's milk should not be given as a drink before your child is a year old, when whole milk can be introduced. Lowfat cow's milk can be given as a drink from two years old, although skim is not recommended before five years, since it lacks the fat and calories a growing child requires.

Sweet foods

Babies have a naturally sweet tooth and the sweetness of breast milk may be partly the reason for this. There's nothing wrong with the occasional sweet treat, but sugar can lead to tooth decay when the milk teeth start to come through. Honey is a sugar too and causes the same problems. It also very occasionally contains a bacteria that has been known to cause infant botulism. Honey is therefore not recommended for babies under one year—after this age the intestines mature and the bacteria is unable to grow.

Salty foods

Don't add salt to food for babies, because their kidneys are insufficiently mature to cope. If you are cooking for the whole family, separate your child's portion before adding any salt. If you do decide your child needs extra salt, add it for them. Salt is added to many commercial foods, and stocks and yeast-based spreads can contain excessive amounts, so look for low-salt alternatives or use them sparingly. Remember too that even "natural" foods such as cheese contains a relatively high proportion of salt.

Natural iron

Babies are born with a store of iron and the mineral is also found in breast and formula milk. However, from about six months, most babies have used up their iron reserves, and even if they are drinking iron-fortified milk, it is important to include foods rich in the mineral in their diet. Children should be given plenty of lean red meat, egg yolks, green vegetables, beans and lentils, and whole-grain or iron-fortified cereals such as rice, barley, or oats.

New tastes

Once your baby is happy with eating first foods, it's time to introduce a wider range of ingredients and increase the number of meals from one to two, and then three. You can now include different grains, lean meat, poultry, dairy products, beans and lentils, and well-cooked egg yolks.

If your baby is happily taking solids, you will probably find that he or she can now eat many family meals, but avoid highly spiced or seasoned foods. Remove a baby-size portion of what you are eating before spicing or seasoning the remainder of the meal.

At this stage, it's a good idea to familiarize your baby with a wider range of flavors, and you will definitely reap the benefits in the future. Lean meat, poultry, beans and lentils, and other vegetarian alternatives combine well with other foods, especially those with stronger flavors. They also have a pleasing texture that will appeal to your baby and take little time to prepare. However, make sure you mash beans and lentils well and use only in small quantities, since they are high in fiber and can be difficult to digest.

Crème fraîche, sour cream, and yogurt lend themselves well to both sweet and savory dishes and add a delicious creaminess to pasta sauces, soups, and stews. Egg yolks must be well cooked and mashed or very finely chopped to avoid the risk of your baby choking.

Pasta can be served in various guises and is a good starting point when meal planning.

From six months, your baby's iron stores start to deplete, so it's important to include sources of iron in his or her diet (see page 11). Vitamin C-rich foods and drinks can enhance iron absorption, so it is advisable to offer them at the same time to help ensure the best effect.

Three meals a day

There are no hard and fast rules when it comes to how much your baby should eat, but the general guideline is 1–4 tablespoons of food per mealtime. However, don't panic if your baby eats more or less than this. Babies seem to thrive on routine and for this reason it is a good idea to introduce three meals a day, plus a couple of healthy snacks. Once feeding is established, try offering mashed or ground foods in place of purées. These encourage your baby to chew, even if milk teeth are yet to come through.

Milk and drinks

You will find that as your baby's appetite increases, his or her need for milk will decline. Around generous 2–2¹/₂ cups of breast milk or formula per day is recommended, but once solid feeding is established, it is advisable to stop giving milk before a meal, since it can suppress the appetite. Continue to give milk at waking and bedtime, but at mealtimes you can also provide water or diluted fresh fruit juice (one part juice to ten parts water) in a lidded feeding cup. After six months, tap water does not need to be boiled, but be sure to use cooled boiled water to make up formula. Still avoid giving cow's milk as a drink, although it is now suitable for cooking.

Infant formula based on goat's milk is unsuitable for babies, and should not be given to children under one year old. Soy-based infant formulas should only be given to babies on the advice of a medical practitioner.

Finger foods

Finger foods help to comfort sore gums and also give your baby a chance to use his or her hands and to practice chewing. Small pieces of ripe banana and bite-size soft-cooked peas can also provide snacks. Lightly toasted bread or bagels that are cut up, well-cooked pasta, low-sugar O-shaped cereals, and teething crackers provide new textures.

Cooking for your baby

Ideally, every morsel that passes your baby's lips should be home-prepared, but this is unrealistic for most of us. However, it's vital to provide as much fresh, unprocessed food as possible, and it's also more economical to make your own.

Many of us fall into the trap of believing that our baby will prefer to eat so-called children's food, and consequently we pander to these expectations by buying foods that we would not normally even contemplate buying or eating ourselves.

Experts firmly believe that good eating habits are formed early, so it's important for parents to provide a variety of foods, encompassing a wide range of flavors, colors, and textures.

Commercial foods

Lack of time and energy leads many of us to resort to the easy option. However, now is not the time to feel guilty—the occasional package or jar will not harm a baby's health, but relying on these foods 100 percent might. When buying commercial baby foods, it is advisable to check the label for unwanted additives, sugars (sucrose, dextrose, glucose), artificial sweeteners (aspartame, saccharin), salt, and thickeners such as modified starch, which simply bulk out the ingredients. Instead opt for brands—especially the organic ones—that are free from additives and do not have added salt, sugar, and sweeteners. There are ranges of frozen organic baby meals now available that come as close as you can get to the quality of home-prepared foods.

Allergies

Statistics show that the number of children with food intolerances is on the rise, yet it is also true that life-threatening allergies are rare. In children, the most commonly responsible foods are cow's milk, gluten, eggs, fish and shellfish, peanuts, tomatoes, sugar, and strawberries, with symptoms ranging from rashes, upset stomachs, and hyperactivity to asthma, eczema, breathing difficulties, and swelling of the throat. It is therefore recommended to introduce the common allergenic foods one at a time and monitor to see if there is any adverse response.

If you have a history of food allergies in the family or suspect a problem with a particular food, it is advisable to talk to your health practitioner as soon as possible. It is also important to read food labels thoroughly and avoid giving suspect foods to children from "atopic" or allergic families until they are at least three years old.

Nut and seed allergy

Although allergies to nuts and seeds are uncommon, the number of children affected does appear to be on the increase. If there is a history of allergies within the immediate family, or if you are worried about peanut allergies, mothers should avoid peanuts or related foods while pregnant or breast-feeding and should not give their child peanuts or related foods until they are at least three years old. If there are no cases of allergies within the family, there is no need for children over one year old to avoid nuts as long as they are slivered, or crushed. Whole nuts are not recommended for children under five years old.

Vegetarian diet

If you bring your child up as a vegetarian, it's important that their diet is balanced. As your child grows, make sure they eat fruit, dairy products, eggs, vegetables, nuts, seeds, beans, and lentils in their daily meals. Be sure your child is getting enough B vitamins, particularly B12, and iron and zinc:

▶ B12: cheese, eggs, fortified foods such as yeast extract and breakfast cereals, textured vegetable protein.

▶ Iron: beans, lentils, whole grains, molasses, leafy green vegetables, dairy products, fortified breakfast cereals, brown rice, and dried fruit.

▶ Zinc: dairy, beans, lentils, nuts, seeds, whole grains, and yeast-based foods.

First birthday

Many babies are able to eat the same foods as the rest of the family and are accustomed to chewing small pieces of food by their first birthday. It is also not uncommon for babies to become more fussy about what they eat around this time. Good eating habits are formed early, so stick with it and get your baby used to experiencing a variety of foods—encompassing a wide range of flavors, colors, and textures.

Many parents and carers have preconceived ideas that babies and toddlers prefer bland foods, yet university researchers have discovered that they are far more open to new tastes and stronger flavors than previously thought—although go easy on overly spicy foods for babies.

While it's not always feasible for the whole family to eat together, you will reap the benefits when you do, even if you manage communal mealtimes only at weekends. Although the target is to encourage your child to eat the same foods as the rest of the family, a high-fiber, lowfat diet is unsuitable for young children. Instead, provide a good balance of high-energy, nutrient-dense foods, including plenty of fruit and vegetables, full-fat dairy produce, bread, pasta, potatoes, and rice, as well as protein foods in the form of lean meat, poultry, white fish, beans and lentils, eggs, and different vegetarian alternatives.

Three meals a day

Babies seem to thrive on routine and because their stomachs are small they require three meals, plus a couple of healthy snacks, a day. Ideally, and if convenient, the main meal of the day should be at lunchtime. Babies seem to be more open to new tastes at this time of day, when they are alert and less fractious—the same could be said of parents! Coarsely mashed, grated, and chopped foods will help your child's teeth and allow him or her to practice chewing. Once your baby is on the move, you will probably have to increase the amount of food you give—babies have high energy requirements for their size.

Fussy eating

Your child will inevitably refuse to even try some foods at times, but the best way to deal with picky eating is to ignore it, however difficult or frustrating it may be. Babies of this age (and toddlers) are often too busy or distracted to sit down and eat. One simple way around this is to give your child his or her own spoon and a bowl containing a little food, while you simultaneously feed your child the main part of the meal—smaller portions are less off-putting too.

Finger foods are also popular and can offer some relief to babies who are teething. Lightly steamed sticks of vegetables or peeled raw fruit are ideal for sore gums, especially if they are chilled. Thin slices of bread, slowly dried in the oven, are a healthy alternative to commercial teething crackers, which can contain added sugar and other additives. Slices of pita bread, muffins, naan bread, and tortilla can be dipped into vegetable or lentil purées or chickpea dip.

Make sure that you never leave a baby unattended while eating because of the possible risk of choking.

Milk and drinks

Milk remains an important source of nutrients and your baby still requires about a generous 2–2^1/$_2$ cups of milk a day. Whole cow's milk, goat's milk, or sheep's milk can be given as a drink from one year. While you may still be breast-feeding, it is no longer necessary to provide formula milk, although you can of course continue to do so if your baby is not eating particularly well yet and you are concerned that he or she is not getting the nutrients needed.

Water is the best alternative drink to milk. Some bottled waters have mineral contents that are unsuitable for babies. However, there are bottled waters that are suitable for infants and are labeled accordingly.

Fresh fruit juices are a good source of vitamin C, which helps our bodies absorb iron from a meal, but it's best to dilute them (one part juice to ten parts water) and give them in a beaker or cup rather than a bottle, to reduce potential damage to teeth from the sugar.

18–36 months

What does my toddler need?

Children over a year old can enjoy the same meals as adults, but their requirement for high-energy foods is much greater as they continue to grow and develop. They are usually very active at this age, which means that they constantly need the calories and the energy these foods provide, yet a varied, healthy, balanced diet will also provide all the nutrients your toddler needs.

The term "balanced diet" can intimidate even the most nutritionally aware parent. Yet as long as your child is eating a good mix of foods on a regular basis, he or she should be getting all the nutrients necessary. Obviously, the range of foods will vary depending on special diets, eating preferences, and the presence of food allergies or intolerances, but remember to include the following daily:

▶ Starchy foods—these include low-sugar breakfast cereals, bread, pasta, rice, and potatoes. Aim for about four servings a day, because these foods are an excellent source of energy, fiber, vitamins, and minerals. Remember, however, that toddlers find it

difficult to digest large amounts of high-fiber foods such as whole-wheat bread and brown rice. Fiber can also interfere with the absorption of certain minerals.

▶ Fruits and vegetables—fresh, frozen, dried, and canned—provide rich amounts of vitamins, minerals, and beneficial plant nutrients. Try to offer your child four to five different types of fresh produce a day.

▶ Meat, poultry, fish (if there is no risk of allergies), eggs, beans and lentils, tofu, and nuts (if there is no risk of allergies) are protein-rich foods essential for growth and development. They should be included once or twice a day. If your toddler is vegetarian, give one to two servings of beans or lentils a day. Oily fish, including tuna and salmon, provide omega-3 essential fatty acids, which have been found to benefit the brain, eyes, and skin. You can give boys up to four portions of oily fish a week and girls up to two.

▶ Dairy foods—whole milk, cheese, and yogurt provide protein, vitamins, and minerals, including calcium for healthy teeth and bones. Cow's, goat's, and sheep's milk are suitable as a drink from one year. You can use lowfat milk from two years if your child is eating well and has a varied diet.

What to avoid

▸ Most young children naturally have a sweet tooth, but try not to pander to this—sweet food will spoil a child's appetite as well as lead to tooth decay. Nevertheless, an outright ban can backfire, making them even more desirable! Don't resort to foods that replace sugar with artificial sweeteners, since they can cause an upset stomach if eaten in excess, and still encourage a sweet tooth.

▸ Don't add salt to your toddler's food—the seasoning is found naturally in many foods and commercial products anyway. Between the ages of one and three years, children should have no more than 2 g of salt a day.

▸ Raw eggs, and foods that contain raw or partially cooked eggs such as homemade mayonnaise, are best avoided because of the risk of salmonella poisoning.

▸ Shark, swordfish, and marlin can contain relatively high levels of mercury, which might adversely affect a child's nervous system.

▸ Whole nuts for children under five years of age are not recommended.

Drinks

Milk should still form an important part of your child's diet, since it provides energy, protein, calcium, iron, zinc, and vitamins.

Cola, tea, and coffee are best avoided due to their caffeine content, while sweetened fruit juices, sodas, and squash are high in sugar and acidity. Sugar-laden drinks can decay teeth and curb the appetite, leading to poor weight gain. However, low-sugar alternatives that contain artificial sweeteners are often no better: they encourage a sweet tooth and can upset the stomach if drunk in excess.

Water, diluted fresh fruit juice, and homemade fruit juices are the preferred option. Smoothies, made from puréed fruit, milk and/or yogurt, freshly squeezed juices, and homemade hot chocolate (cubes of good-quality chocolate melted into hot milk) all make nutritious drinks that are not full of sugar or additives. Serve in a feeder cup or plastic cup, not in a bottle.

Iron

Iron deficiency can be common among women, teenage girls, and children. The mineral is essential for the healthy development of mind and body, and a deficiency can lead to tiredness, irritability, poor concentration, anemia, and a compromised immune system. Iron absorption can be enhanced by accompanying a meal with a glass of diluted orange juice, or fruit and vegetables. Red meat and liver (pâté), fish, eggs, beans and lentils, some fruit and vegetables, whole-grain cereals, fortified breakfast cereals, and dried fruit are all good sources of iron.

Establish a routine

Work on establishing a regular eating pattern, based on three main meals, plus a couple of healthy snacks a day. Even this can take time and patience to establish, however, so don't panic. There is no need to purée or mash foods—your toddler should be getting used to chewing foods by now. Some young children dislike "lumps," whether meat, fish, fruit, or vegetables, and very finely chopping or grinding such foods may make them more acceptable.

If "grazing" is preferred by your toddler, take advantage of this by offering a varied selection of healthy snacks—this may be a way of supplementing an otherwise restricted diet. As long as your toddler is gaining weight and also growing and developing well, then there should be no need for concern.

The following ideas may help when you are faced with a hungry toddler:

- Slices of fruit and vegetables (fresh or canned), including melon, papaya, apricot, plums and citrus fruits, broccoli, and cauliflower

- Rice cakes with low-salt yeast extract

- Fruit muffins with banana

- French toast

- Plain low-fat yogurt with fresh fruit purée

- Whole-wheat bread with smooth, thinly spread peanut butter

- Breadsticks with chickpea dip

- Soft tortilla with guacamole or cream cheese

- Oat-style cookies

- Slices of pineapple with cream cheese

- Dried fruit such as apples, apricots, peaches, pears, dates, pitted prunes, raisins (soaked until soft so they do not pose a choking hazard)

- Vegetable chips or no-salt chips

- Fruit cookies

- Drop cookies

- Banana sandwich

- Sliced or grated cheese with crackers

Presentation

Imaginative and attractive presentation can make the difference between a child eating or refusing even to try a meal. This doesn't mean you have to spend hours painstakingly arranging every meal on a plate, but try to make meals look as inviting as possible by including foods of different colors, textures, and shapes. Interesting plates, eating utensils, bibs, and mats can make all the difference, as can a special theme.

Outside influences

Many toddlers attend a pre-school and with this comes its own challenges. You may be fortunate to find an ideal establishment that serves a variety of freshly prepared, nutritious lunches, snacks, and healthy drinks. Realistically, however, food standards tend to vary and it can be awkward for parents to ask for changes without appearing difficult and demanding. Many pre-schools are open to parents providing their own drinks, snacks, and packed lunches and this may be a welcome option.

Alternatively, take the softly-softly approach, arming yourself with relevant information, articles, and books. Often a lack of knowledge is to blame for poor food quality and all that is needed is a little encouragement.

Eating out

It can be a challenge to find a restaurant that not only welcomes children with open arms but also provides decent, healthy food. Most children's menus offer the usual repertoire of chicken and fries, or burger and fries, followed by poor-quality ice cream and jello. There is also the further lure of a free gift!

Consequently, all your good intentions fly out of the window.

Most children love the novelty of eating out and, from experience, the better-quality pizza chains, Italian, Indian, and Chinese restaurants offer the best choice and are often more welcoming to families with young children. Alternatively, choose an appetizer from the main menu or ask for a separate plate and share your meal. Sometimes the chef may provide a small, child-size portion of an entrée.

Eating out can be a hit-or-miss affair, and it's best to pick a time when your little one is not very tired and choose a restaurant that's not too formal, otherwise it may be difficult to relax. To prevent occasional boredom, take along pens and paper or a small toy to help keep your child entertained.

Coping with a fussy eater

All children go through stages of picky eating and their appetites can be equally unpredictable. However frustrating this may be, try not to let this trouble you. There are plenty of stories of toddlers surviving on a limited diet for some unimaginable amount of time—remarkably, most don't seem to suffer long-term ill effects.

How do you encourage your child to eat the right foods, and what do you do if he or she refuses to eat at all? There are no easy answers, but the following guidelines should help you cope more easily with those challenging times.

▸ Don't force your child to eat. Conflict and tension serve only to make the situation worse and may lead to your child using mealtimes as a way of seeking attention. Children are remarkably clever at picking up on the anxieties of their parents and may well tune in to your own insecurities about food. Instead, gently try to coax or encourage your child to try a little bit of what you have prepared. You may find that your child will happily eat a meal once you've encouraged him or her to try just a mouthful.

▸ If your gentle coaxing doesn't work, remove the food without making a fuss, but don't offer an alternative dish, however hard this may be. It's important that a child learns to eat what's on offer rather than expect endless alternatives.

▸ Don't overload your child's plate. Small amounts of food tend to be more acceptable.

▸ Praise and encourage your child as much as possible, even if he or she eats only one or two mouthfuls.

▸ Don't let your child fill up on juice or other drinks between meals—some children confuse hunger with thirst.

- Sticker charts are an incredibly simple yet effective means of encouraging good eating habits. You can buy them or make your own, choosing stickers based on your child's favorite cartoon characters or pastimes.

- Make eating fun. Picnics, even if it's only a cloth arranged on the kitchen floor, or games, or basing a meal on a theme such as a favorite cartoon character, book, or season can be a real success.

- Try to ignore poor eating habits and complaints such as "Yuck!", however hard this may be.

- Ask a friend of your child's who you know to be a good eater to come to dinner. Children often learn by example and may be encouraged to eat by their peers. But beware, this can sometimes backfire—some children refuse to eat certain foods just because a friend dislikes them!

- Don't fall into the trap of bribing your child with a dessert, and then giving it even if the main meal remains uneaten. This will only help to discourage good eating habits. Similarly, try not to use sweet foods as a reward for finishing savories—however tempting this may be!

- Compromise is sometimes the only way to get your child to eat certain things. Combine foods that you know your child likes with others that are untried or previously rejected.

4 years plus

For most children, their fifth year heralds the start of part- or full-time education. School presents its own challenges and it can be a time when good intentions and eating habits fall by the wayside. However, a nutritious, varied diet is as important as ever—sustaining and boosting energy levels, helping concentration, and even assisting brain power.

Nutritional needs

Children under the age of five need a diet higher in fat and lower in fiber than adults do, but at this age they should be eating a diet similar in content to that recommended for their parents or carers. We all need energy (calories), protein, carbohydrates, the right types of fat, vitamins, and minerals for the body and mind to function properly.

▸ Bread, potatoes, rice, pasta, and other cereals should form the main part of every meal. Whole-grain cereals supply fiber and nutrients and should be included in larger amounts.

▸ Fruit and vegetables (fresh, frozen, and canned) are crucial to good health, and a child should eat five servings a day. A serving is the amount a child can fit in one hand, but also includes a glass of fresh fruit juice per day.

▸ Meat, poultry, fish, beans and lentils, eggs, nuts, and tofu are vital for the body's growth and repair. Provide a variety of these protein foods once or twice a day, and include one portion of oily fish at least once a week.

▸ Dairy products, including cheese, milk, and yogurt should be eaten several times a day. Children over five can be given lowfat varieties as long as they are eating a good and varied diet.

▸ The consumption of foods high in sugar and saturated or hydrogenated fat, such as cakes, cookies, chips, candies, or sodas, should be limited.

Three meals a day

It may be clichéd, but breakfast really is the most important meal of the day, since it replenishes nutrients and energy reserves depleted overnight. It is now widely recognized that children who eat a decent breakfast perform better at school and have improved concentration and energy levels. A balance of carbohydrate and protein foods (cereal and milk, oatmeal with fruit, egg and toast) will provide sustained energy and keep blood sugar levels on an even keel.

Salt

Try and keep the intake of salt as low as possible.

▸ 4 to 6 years—maximum 3 g a day

▸ 7 to 10 years—maximum 5 g a day

▸ 11 years upward—maximum 6 g a day

(Source: Food and Drink Federation)

School lunches

School lunches vary in quality and choice, depending on where you live, and a packed lunch may be the best way of ensuring that your child is getting a nutritious lunch—that is, as long as it's eaten!

Here are some simple ideas for sandwiches and fillings:

▸ Bagel with cream cheese

▸ Tortilla with sliced cooked chicken, guacamole, and lettuce

▸ Peanut butter with mashed banana

▸ Pita bread with tuna, avocado, mayonnaise, scallion, and a squeeze of lemon juice

▸ Coleslaw and grated Cheddar cheese

▸ Chickpea dip, diced tomato, and alfalfa sprouts

▸ Ham, chopped, hard-cooked egg, and mayonnaise

▸ Ham, chopped pineapple, and cottage cheese

▸ Broiled chicken slices with berries

▸ Hard-cooked egg with yogurt

▸ Sliced turkey with soy chips

▸ Cheddar cheese with grated apple

▸ Grated carrot and cream cheese

Other ideas:

▸ Fruit and vegetable sticks with dip

▸ Fruit muffins with cream cheese

▸ Breadsticks and vegetable sticks with chickpea dip

▸ Fruit dessert with fresh fruit

▸ Banana topped with plain yogurt

▸ Banana bread with cream cheese

▸ Slice of quiche or pizza

▸ Bowl of salad greens with separate dressing

▸ Potato or pasta salad

▸ Rice cakes with banana

▸ Homemade popcorn

▸ Dried fruit

Even if your child has a cooked school lunch, it's best to provide a decent meal at the end of the day to ensure that he or she is getting the full range of foods and nutrients needed. Eating together, if possible, encourages children to eat a wider variety of foods as well as enjoy the social aspect of sharing mealtimes.

Drinks

Drinking enough fluids is as essential for concentration, clarity of thought, and energy levels as eating well—a 2 percent loss in body fluids, for example, can cause a 20 percent reduction in mental and physical performance. Most children don't drink enough, especially at school, and although the amount of fluids they need depends on age and weight, a guide is:

▸ 5 glasses a day for 4–6-year-olds

▸ 6 glasses a day for 7–10-year-olds

Avoid sugary sodas, tea, and coffee and opt instead for water, diluted fresh fruit juice, smoothies, or milk.

6–9 months

Weaning is the gradual process of reducing a baby's total dependence on milk to eating a full and varied diet, which will eventually be the same as the rest of the family. Begin slowly by introducing simple purées, then start to offer a wider range of foods in the subsequent few weeks.

During this period you'll notice changes in your baby. He or she will probably cut a few teeth and will start to sit up, first in a bouncy chair or propped up, and finally progressing to a high chair. This increasing independence is also displayed in your baby's eating habits. Your baby will enjoy using his or her hands and eating finger foods.

Meal Planner

6 to 8 months: coarsely puréed food.

8 to 9 months: mashed or ground foods.

Drinks: breast or formula milk, water, and diluted unsweetened non-citrus fruit juice.

Suitable foods: fruit, soft-cooked or shredded vegetables, grains, small amounts of protein from dairy products such as hard cheese, and cow's milk (in cooking), well-cooked egg yolks, lentils, beans, chicken, and meat.

Avoid: cow's milk (as a drink), nuts, soy, fish, shellfish, soft or bleu cheese, chilies, salt, honey, overly spicy food, raw eggs and egg whites, and sugar.

	EARLY MORNING	BREAKFAST	SLEEP	LUNCH	SLEEP	DINNER	BEDTIME
DAY 1	MILK	Baby Rice with apple purée	MILK	Carrot Purée; Pear Purée & yogurt	MILK	Avocado Purée; toasted bagel, cut up; mashed banana & yogurt	MILK
DAY 2	MILK	No- or low-sugar cereal & mashed banana	MILK	Chicken & Pineapple Cheese; lightly toasted bagel, cut up; apple purée	MILK	Well-cooked egg yolks; toast slices; yogurt & Pear Purée	MILK
DAY 3	MILK	Apricot & Rutabaga Purée; toast slices	MILK	Finely ground chicken, baby cereal; Orchard Fruit Purée	MILK	Pastina with Butternut Squash; chickpea dip; yogurt & mashed fruit	MILK
DAY 4	MILK	Apricot Oatmeal; Pear Purée	MILK	Minestrone Soup, toast slices; mashed banana	MILK	Cauliflower, Potato & Leek Purée; Mango & Yogurt Purée	MILK
DAY 5	MILK	No- or low-sugar cereal & mashed banana	MILK	Bean & Root Vegetable Mash; baby cereal & apple purée	MILK	Minestrone Soup; well-cooked egg yolks; Chicken & Pineapple Cheese	MILK
DAY 6	MILK	Apricot Oatmeal; toast slices	MILK	Pastina with Butternut Squash; Broccoli & Pea Purée; yogurt	MILK	Bean & Root Vegetable Mash, cottage cheese; Pear Purée	MILK
DAY 7	MILK	Baby Rice & Pear Purée	MILK	Finely ground pork; toast slices; Orchard Fruit Purée & yogurt	MILK	Broccoli & Pea Purée, chickpea dip; Mango & Yogurt Purée	MILK

NOTE *The above meal planner is a general guide to the gradual introduction of solids for a baby of six months. Start off giving simple purées of vegetables (carrots, squashes) and fruit (pears, apples), then begin to extend the choice to darker vegetables and widen the variety of fruits. Add mashed meats and poultry, wheat products, and egg yolks. Introduce all foods on a gradual basis to enable your baby's digestive system to adjust to solids.*

Baby Rice

15 Portions   Baby rice is a good introduction to solid foods.

scant ¼ cup white short-grain rice

breast or formula milk

Rinse the rice under cold running water and drain. **Put** in a pan and add enough cold water just to cover it. **Bring** to a boil and stir. Reduce the heat, then **cover** and let simmer for 15–20 minutes, or until the water has been absorbed and the grains are very tender.

Purée the rice in a blender with a little breast or formula milk until smooth.

Pear Purée

2–3 Portions   Pears make a perfect first purée because they are one of the least allergenic of foods.

1 small, ripe pear

2 tbsp water

Wash, **peel**, **core**, and **chop** the pear. **Put** the pear in a pan with the water. **Bring** to a boil and cook for 5–8 minutes, or until tender. **Cool**, then purée the pear in a blender until smooth, adding a little of the cooking water if necessary.

Carrot Purée

1–2 Portions   Carrots' sweetness makes this a popular first food.

1 small carrot

1–2 tbsp water

Scrape or peel the carrot, then slice. **Steam** the carrot for 10 minutes, or until tender. **Cool**, then purée the carrot in a blender until smooth, adding a little of the cooking water if necessary.

Avocado Purée

1 Portion Choose ripe, unblemished fruit for this purée.

½ small avocado

Peel and pit the avocado, then scoop out the flesh with a spoon. Mash the avocado with a fork until smooth and creamy. Serve immediately before the flesh browns and discolors.

Orchard Fruit Purée

6–8 Portions Once your baby enjoys single vegetable and fruit purées, try to introduce new flavors.

1 small dessert apple

1 small, ripe pear

1 small, ripe peach

Wash, peel, core, and pit the fruit, then chop into small pieces. Steam or boil the apple and pear for 5 minutes, or until soft.

Cool, then mash all the fruit or purée in a blender until smooth, adding a little of the cooking water if necessary.

Broccoli & Pea Purée

2–3 Portions You can use breast or formula milk instead of the water to reduce any bitterness in the broccoli.

3 broccoli florets

handful of frozen peas

Steam or boil the broccoli for 7–10 minutes, adding the peas 3 minutes before the end of the cooking time.

Cool, then mash the broccoli and peas or purée in a blender until smooth, adding a little of the cooking water if necessary.

Cauliflower, Potato & Leek Purée

4–6 Portions Children's palates are particularly sensitive to bitter foods. Certain vegetables such as cauliflower and broccoli can be slightly bitter, which is best reduced by combining them with dairy products such as milk or cheese.

1 potato
½ small leek
3 cauliflower florets
breast or formula milk

Wash, **peel**, and **cube** the potato. **Wash** the leek, remove the tough outer layer, then thinly slice. **Steam** or boil the potato, leek, and cauliflower for 15 minutes, or until tender.

Cool, then purée in a blender with a little breast or formula milk until smooth and creamy.

Apricot & Rutabaga Purée

2–3 Portions It is a good idea to encourage your baby to try a range of fruit and vegetable combinations, because he or she will then be less likely to be a fussy eater in the future—well, that's the theory!

1 wedge of rutabaga
2 fresh, ripe apricots

Wash, **peel**, and **cube** the wedge of rutabaga. **Halve** the apricots and then pit them carefully. **Steam** or boil the rutabaga for 15 minutes, or until tender, **adding** the apricots 5 minutes before the end of the cooking time.

Cool, then peel off the apricot skin. **Purée** the flesh in a blender until smooth, adding a little of the cooking water if necessary.

Minestrone Soup

4 Portions This classic Italian soup is a nutritious combination of beans, pasta, and vegetables, providing a good range of vitamins and minerals.

1 tbsp olive oil

½ small onion, finely chopped

1 small carrot, peeled and diced

1 bay leaf

¼ cup no-salt or low-salt
  vegetable bouillon

4 tbsp passata (strained tomatoes)

½ cup small pasta shapes

4 tbsp canned, no-salt, no-sugar Great
  Northern beans, drained and rinsed

½ cup spinach, washed and thick stalks
  removed, finely chopped

2 tbsp freshly grated Parmesan cheese

Heat the olive oil in a heavy-bottomed saucepan. **Add** the onion and carrot and cook over a medium heat for 8–10 minutes, **stirring** occasionally, until the vegetables have softened.

Add the bay leaf, bouillon, and passata, then bring to a boil. **Reduce** the heat, cover, and simmer for 15 minutes, or until the vegetables are tender.

Add the pasta and beans, then bring the soup back to a boil and **simmer** until the pasta is tender. **Stir** occasionally to prevent the pasta sticking.

Add the spinach and cook until tender. **Remove** the bay leaf, **stir** in the cheese, and purée, mash, or chop the mixture, depending on your baby's age.

Apricot Oatmeal

4 Portions   This recipe is a dessert that can double up as a breakfast. This is worth remembering if you have plenty left over. The dried apricots are cooked and puréed and are delicious with yogurt. Cooked and puréed dates make a delicious alternative.

6 unsulfured dried, ready-to-eat apricots

8 tbsp porridge oats

breast milk or formula milk

Wash and soak the apricots in cold water overnight. The next day, drain the apricots and place in a pan. Cover with water and bring to a boil, then reduce the heat and simmer for 10–15 minutes, until soft.

Purée the cooked apricots in a blender until smooth, adding a little of the cooking water if necessary.

Meanwhile, cover the oats with half water and half milk. Bring to a boil, reduce the heat and simmer for 5–8 minutes, until the oats are tender and creamy. Combine with some or all of the apricot purée.

Chicken & Pineapple Cheese

4 Portions Finger foods are a great way to encourage babies to chew and also enable them to feed themselves. Slices of toast, pita, bagels, teething crackers, or breadsticks are perfect with this creamy dip.

1 tsp olive oil

2 oz/55 g skinless chicken breast

4 tbsp cottage cheese

1–2 tbsp plain yogurt

1 slice of fresh pineapple, peeled, cored, and diced

Heat the oil in a nonstick skillet. Add the chicken breast and cook, turning occasionally, for 12–15 minutes, or until golden and cooked through. Set aside to cool to room temperature, then very finely chop the chicken.

Combine the chicken with the cottage cheese, yogurt, and pineapple and mash together. Alternatively, put all the ingredients in a blender and whiz the mixture to a coarse purée.

Bean & Root Vegetable Mash

4 Portions   This comforting combination is a favorite with little ones and adults alike. For young infants, the beans should be creamed or puréed until smooth.

Cook the potato and yellow turnip in boiling water for 15–20 minutes, or until tender. Drain and purée or cream with the olive oil and butter.

Heat the beans through and mash or chop, depending on the age of your child. Peel the egg and discard the white. Mash the egg yolk and combine with the beans and creamed potato.

1 medium potato, peeled and cubed

scant 1 cup yellow turnip or celery root, peeled and cubed

1 tsp olive oil

small knob of sweet butter or margarine

4 tbsp no-salt, no-sugar baked beans

1 hard-cooked egg yolk

4–6 Portions This nurturing dish is a favorite weaning food in Italy. When your infant is older and ready for more substantial dishes, slightly larger pasta shapes can be substituted.

Pastina with Butternut Squash

6 oz/175 g butternut squash, peeled, seeded, and chopped

3 oz/85 g dried baby pasta shapes or pastina

small piece of unsalted butter

1 tsp olive oil

2 tbsp freshly grated Parmesan cheese

Steam the butternut squash for about 10–15 minutes, or until tender, then purée or mash with a fork.

Meanwhile, cook the pasta in a pan of boiling water according to the package directions, then drain well and return to the pan. Add the butter, oil, and Parmesan cheese and stir until the pasta is coated, then combine with the butternut squash.

Mango & Yogurt Purée

2 Portions   You could replace the mango in this recipe with pear or orchard fruits. The wheat germ is a good source of fiber, vitamins, and minerals for your child, but it can be left out of the recipe if preferred.

Steam the mango for 2 minutes or, if very ripe, **mash** with a fork and press through a strainer until smooth. **Mix** well with the yogurt and wheat germ.

½ small, ripe mango, peeled, seeded, and chopped

4–6 tbsp plain yogurt

1 tsp wheat germ

9–12 months

This can be a challenging but rewarding stage in a baby's development. Specially prepared meals may be needed less, and your baby may start to enjoy the social aspect of eating with the rest of the family. At this stage, babies will also begin to exercise their desire for independence and a growing curiosity for what's around them. This can prove an interesting time, and plenty of patience and a sense of humor are the key to preserving your sanity!

Meal Planner

9 to 10 months: ground foods.

10 to 12 months: finely chopped foods.

Drinks: breast or formula milk, water, and diluted unsweetened non-citrus fruit juice.

Suitable foods: fruit, soft-cooked or shredded vegetables, meat, chicken, hard cheese, yogurt, grains, lentils, beans, and egg yolks.

Avoid: raw eggs and egg whites, fish, shellfish, nuts, peanut butter, soy, honey, chilies, salt, overly spicy food, cow's milk (as a drink), citrus fruits, and soft and bleu cheese.

	BREAKFAST	MID-MORNING	LUNCH	DINNER	BEDTIME
DAY 1	Baby Rice & fruit purée; toast slices; milk	MILK	Macaroni & cheese; broccoli; Apple & Plum Yogurt	Chicken & Apple Bites; mashed vegetables & new potatoes; Fruit Sherbet	MILK
DAY 2	Well-cooked egg yolks; broiled tomatoes; toast slices; milk	MILK	Ham & Pineapple Rice, peas; Mango & Yogurt Purée	Cheese & Potato Casserole; diced vegetables; lightly toasted bagel, cut up; stewed apple	MILK
DAY 3	No- or low-sugar cereal & banana slices; milk	MILK	Vegetable & Pasta Cheese; chickpea dip; stewed apple & yogurt	Spring Vegetable Risotto, toast slices; Apple & Plum Yogurt	MILK
DAY 4	Apricot Oatmeal; Orchard Fruit Purée; milk	MILK	Pastina with Butternut Squash; toast slices; diced fruit & yogurt	Ham & Pineapple Rice; diced, well-cooked carrot; Fruit Sherbet	MILK
DAY 5	No- or low-sugar cereal; diced fruit; milk	MILK	Minestrone Soup, lightly toasted bagel, cut up; oat-style cookies & diced fruit	Vegetable & Pasta Cheese; peas; Orchard Fruit Purée & yogurt	MILK
DAY 6	Baby Rice & fruit purée; toast slices; milk	MILK	Pink Pasta Salad; cottage cheese; Apple & Plum Yogurt	Creamy Tomato & Lentil Soup; lightly toasted bagel, cut up; stewed fruit	MILK
DAY 7	Well-cooked egg yolks; broiled tomatoes; toast slices; milk	MILK	Cheese & Potato Casserole; diced, well-cooked carrot; stewed apple	Spring Vegetable Risotto; cottage cheese; oat-style cookies & diced fruit	MILK

Creamy Tomato & Lentil Soup

6 Portions Remarkably, children who turn their noses up at vegetables will happily eat them when blended into a soup. Most children love a bowl of tomato soup, and this one is free from any additives. The lentils add goodness and substance, but they can be swapped for beans or cooked rice.

generous ⅛ cup red split lentils, rinsed

2 tsp olive oil

1 small onion, chopped

1 small carrot, peeled, and very finely
chopped

1 small celery stalk, chopped

9 oz/250 g carton creamed tomatoes

1¼ cups no-salt or homemade
vegetable stock

cream or plain yogurt, to serve (optional)

cheese toasts

2 slices bread, cut into strips

butter, for spreading

¼ cup grated Gruyère or Cheddar
cheese

pinch of dried oregano,
(optional)

Put the lentils in a pan and cover with water, then bring to a boil. **Reduce** the heat and let simmer, partially covered, for 20–25 minutes, or until tender. **Drain** well and set aside.

While the lentils are cooking, **make** the soup. **Heat** the oil in a heavy-bottom skillet. **Add** the onion, then cover and cook over low heat for 10 minutes, or until softened. **Add** the carrot and celery and cook for an additional 2 minutes, **stirring** occasionally to prevent the vegetables sticking to the bottom of the skillet and burning. **Add** the creamed tomatoes and stock and bring to a boil. **Reduce** the heat and let simmer, partially covered, for 20–25 minutes, or until the vegetables are tender and the liquid has reduced and thickened. **Add** the lentils to the skillet. Carefully **pour** the mixture into a blender or food processor and blend until smooth and creamy. **Swirl** a spoonful of cream or yogurt, if using, over the soup and serve.

For the Cheese Toasts, **preheat** the broiler to high. Lightly **toast** the bread fingers on one side. **Butter** the other side and sprinkle with the cheese, and oregano if using. **Broil** until golden.

4-6 Portions Although broccoli and cauliflower have been used here, this creamy cheese sauce goes well with many different vegetables, especially carrot, yellow turnip, spinach, and leeks. At this stage, cow's milk is fine for using in cooking.

Vegetable & Pasta Cheese

Steam the broccoli and cauliflower for 8–10 minutes, until tender. Cook the pasta according to the instructions on the package, until the pasta is tender, then drain.

Meanwhile, make the cheese sauce. Melt the butter in a small, heavy-bottomed pan over a low heat. Gradually add the flour, beating well to form a smooth paste. Cook for 30 seconds, stirring continuously. Add the milk, a little at a time, whisking well to prevent any lumps forming, then stir in the oregano. Simmer for 2 minutes until smooth and creamy, then mix in the cheese.

Add the cooked cauliflower, broccoli, and pasta to the cheese sauce and stir well. Finely chop or mash the mixture.

4 florets broccoli, cut into smaller florets

4 florets cauliflower, cut into smaller florets

scant 1 cup small penne or farfalle pasta

cheese sauce

1½ tbsp sweet butter or margarine

1 tbsp all-purpose flour

¾ cup whole milk

½ tsp dried oregano

½ cup Cheddar cheese, grated

Ham & Pineapple Rice

2 Portions   A classic combination of ham and pineapple is presented in this baby-friendly dish. Corn kernels are added for sweetness.

Place the rice in a pan. Cover with the water and bring to a boil. Reduce the heat, cover, and simmer for 15 minutes, until the water has been absorbed and the rice is cooked.

Meanwhile, heat the broiler to high. Brush the ham with olive oil and broil for 8–10 minutes on each side, until cooked through. Cut the meat into bite-sized pieces.

At the same time, melt the butter in a small, heavy-bottomed pan and add the corn and pineapple and heat through for a minute or so. Add the rice, ham, and parsley to the pan and stir well to combine.

⅓ cup long-grain rice, rinsed

1 cup water

1 thick ham steak

olive oil, for glazing

2 tbsp sweet butter

3 tbsp corn kernels, drained and rinsed

3 oz/85 g fresh pineapple, cubed

1 tbsp finely chopped fresh parsley

Chicken & Apple Bites

Makes 20 A tasty combination of chicken and apple, mixed with whole-wheat bread crumbs. Make the bites small enough for finger food or cut them up into bite-size pieces.

1 apple, peeled, cored, and grated

2 skinless, boneless chicken breasts,
   cut into chunks

½ red onion, chopped

1 tbsp chopped fresh parsley

scant 1 cup fresh whole-wheat bread crumbs

1 tbsp concentrated chicken stock

whole-wheat flour, for coating

corn or sunflower-seed oil, for pan-frying

Spread the apple out on a clean dish towel or paper towels and press out all the excess moisture.

Put the chicken, apple, onion, parsley, bread crumbs, and stock in a food processor and pulse briefly until well combined.

Spread the flour out on a plate. **Divide** the mixture into 20 or more mini portions, shape each portion into a ball and roll in the flour.

Heat a little oil in a nonstick skillet over medium heat and cook the balls for 5–8 minutes, or until golden brown all over and cooked through. **Remove** and drain on paper towels. Serve hot or cold.

Cheese & Potato Casserole

2–4 Portions This is real comfort food—warming and sustaining. The dish has a center of baby peas and very finely chopped leek, which will introduce your baby to slightly chunkier food.

Cook the potatoes and sweet potatoes in a pan of boiling water for 10 minutes, or until tender.

Meanwhile, **heat** the oil in a small, heavy-bottom skillet and cook the leek, stirring frequently, for 5 minutes, or until softened. **Add** the thyme and baby peas and cook, stirring, for 1 minute. Remove from the heat.

Drain the potatoes and return to the pan. **Add** the butter, milk, and mustard, if using, and **mash** until smooth and creamy, adding more milk if necessary. **Stir** in the cheese.

Preheat the broiler to medium. **Grease** a small, ovenproof dish and spoon half the creamed potato into the dish. **Top** with the leek mixture. **Spoon** the remainder of the creamed potato on top and score the top with a fork. **Cook** under the broiler until the top is beginning to crisp and turn golden. **Let** cool slightly before serving.

5½ oz/150 g potatoes such as Russet, peeled and diced

3 oz/85 g orange-fleshed sweet potatoes, peeled and diced

2 tsp olive oil

1 small leek, very finely chopped

pinch of dried thyme

⅜ cup frozen baby peas

1 tbsp unsalted butter, plus extra for greasing

4–6 tbsp milk

¼ tsp Dijon mustard (optional)

⅓ cup grated sharp Cheddar cheese

Instead of broiling, the creamed potato and vegetable mixture can simply be mixed together in a pan and served alongside the casserole. The creamed potato is popular with children, and makes a good accompaniment to other meat or vegetable dishes.

Pink Pasta Salad

2–4 Portions   Salad may not spring to mind as a suitable infant food but this one may change your ideas, and a fun-shaped pasta will add to its appeal. The choice of salad ingredients can also be varied according to your child's likes and dislikes.

scant 1 cup fun-shaped pasta

½ small red bell pepper, seeded and diced

2 tomatoes, seeded and diced

**2 tbsp canned corn kernels,
    drained and rinsed**

**1–2 slices of ham or 1 cooked sausage,
    diced (optional)**

2 tbsp red pesto

1–2 tbsp store-bought mayonnaise

Cook the pasta according to the instructions on the package, until the pasta is tender. Drain and set aside.

Steam the bell pepper for 2 minutes, until softened.

Place the pasta, bell pepper, tomatoes, corn, and ham, if using, in a bowl. Mix together the pesto and mayonnaise and spoon the mixture over the salad ingredients. Mix everything together well to coat all the ingredients in the sauce.

Spring Vegetable Risotto

4–6 Portions   Rice is perfect for babies because it is comforting and easy to eat. Spring vegetables are used here, but do experiment. Carrots, green beans, fava beans, red bell peppers, onions, or squashes can all be added to this risotto.

1 small leek, peeled and very finely chopped

1 small zucchini, very finely chopped

small handful of frozen peas

small piece of unsalted butter

1 tsp olive oil

generous ⅜ cup risotto rice

1½ cups hot no-salt or homemade vegetable or chicken stock

½ tsp dried oregano

2 tbsp freshly grated Parmesan cheese

Steam the leek and zucchini for 5 minutes, then **add** the peas after 2 minutes and cook until tender.

Melt the butter with the oil in a heavy-bottom skillet. **Add** the rice and **cook**, stirring, for 2–3 minutes, or until the grains are well coated in the butter and oil and are translucent.

Add the stock a ladleful at a time, waiting until it has been absorbed before adding more. Cook over medium-low heat for 20 minutes, stirring constantly. **Add** the oregano, Parmesan cheese, and vegetables and let simmer, stirring, for an additional 5–10 minutes, or until all the liquid has been absorbed and the rice is tender. **Purée** the risotto, then mash it or leave it as it is, depending on your baby's age, adding extra stock or water if it is too thick.

When your baby is very young, it is essential that this dish is properly mashed. However, it is wise to encourage your baby to eat "lumpy" food once he or she is familiar with purées and mashed food or else they may refuse to eat "lumpy" food at a later stage. Chewing also helps the development of speech muscles.

Fruit Sherbet

8 Scoops   This refreshing, fruity ice
is very popular when served in
an ice-cream cone, or you could
pour the mixture into ice-pop molds.

2 ripe mangoes
1¼ cups fresh apple juice
3 tbsp confectioners' sugar

Slice the mango on either side of the large central seed and slice off any flesh around the
seed. Scoop out the flesh and set aside. Repeat with the second mango and put the flesh in a
blender or food processor.

Add the apple juice and sugar and process until blended and smooth. Press through a
strainer to remove any fibers from the mangoes.

Pour the mixture into a freezerproof container with a lid and freeze for 2 hours. Remove
from the freezer and beat with a whisk or fork to break up the ice crystals. Smooth the
surface with the back of a spoon, then return to the freezer and freeze for an additional 2 hours.
Beat again, as before, then freeze until solid.

Remove from the freezer 45 minutes before serving to let the sherbet soften.

Apple & Plum Yogurt

2 Portions   Babies can dislike the texture of plums, so mixing them with apple and yogurt can make them more baby friendly.

Put the apple and plums in a pan with the water. Bring to a boil, then reduce the heat and let simmer, covered, for 5 minutes, or until tender. Remove the plum skins and purée the fruit in a blender or press through a strainer until smooth.

Mix the fruit purée and yogurt together, then sprinkle over the crushed cookie, if using, before serving.

1 small dessert apple, peeled, cored, and chopped

2 ripe plums, pitted

2 tbsp water

4–6 tbsp plain yogurt

1 plain cookie, crushed (optional)

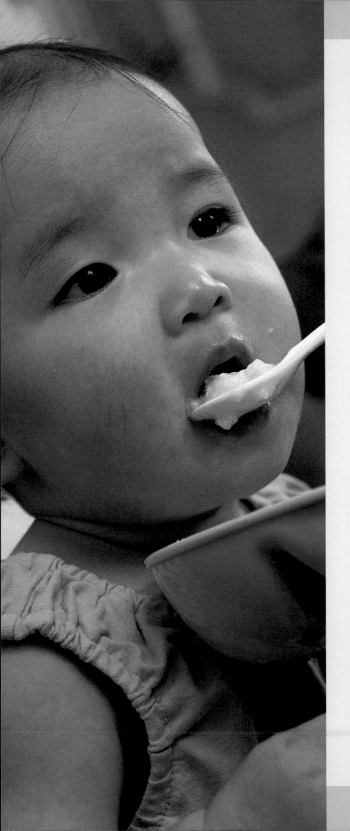

12–18 months

From around his or her first birthday, your baby should be learning to enjoy the same meals as the rest of the family. At this time, babies start to exercise their own independence—and mealtimes are the perfect opportunity! This can be a rewarding but also a frustrating time. Don't worry or make a fuss if your toddler refuses to eat. Most toddlers go through periods of fussy eating, and coaxing and encouragement are undoubtedly far more successful than force-feeding. This approach will also create a more peaceful, harmonious atmosphere for all.

The following recipes cater for four people—two adults and two children—but can easily be halved or doubled, if necessary.

Meal Planner

12 to 14 months: very finely chopped foods.

14 months: chopped foods.

Drinks: breast, formula, or cow's milk (or other alternative), water, and diluted unsweetened fruit (including citrus fruits) or vegetable juice (1 part juice to 10 parts water).

Suitable foods: same as rest of family. Include fish especially boneless white fish (unless allergic).

Avoid: low-fat milk, whole nuts, chilies, salt, overly spicy food, and raw eggs.

	BREAKFAST	LUNCH	DINNER	BEDTIME
DAY 1	Apricot Oatmeal; chopped banana; toast; milk	Creamy Tomato & Lentil Soup; lightly toasted bagel, sliced; yogurt & fruit	Salmon Fish Cakes; sweet potato fries; peas; Fruit Sherbet	MILK
DAY 2	Boiled egg & slices of toast with yeast extract; yogurt & fruit; milk	Cheese & Potato Casserole; chickpea dip; Fruitybocker Glory	Roast Vegetable Lasagna; chickpea dip; Apple & Plum Yogurt	MILK
DAY 3	Cereal; fruit muffin; milk	Rösti Nests, small pieces of vegetables; Mango & Yogurt Purée	White Fish Pasta Bake; vegetables; Strawberry Yogurt Pops	MILK
DAY 4	Poached egg, broiled tomatoes; toast; fruit; milk	Creamy Ham & Peas with Penne; small pieces of broccoli; Apple & Plum Yogurt	Cheese & Potato Casserole; vegetables; Fruitybocker Glory	MILK
DAY 5	Apricot Oatmeal; toast; fruit; milk	Chicken & Apple Bites; vegetables; bananas & yogurt	Ham & Pineapple Rice, vegetables or salad; Quick Summer Surprise	MILK
DAY 6	Boiled egg & slices of toast; chopped banana & yogurt; milk	Ground Beef with Apricots, spiral pasta; Strawberry Yogurt Pops	Rösti Nests, cottage cheese, vegetables; stewed apples & yogurt	MILK
DAY 7	Pancakes with yogurt & fruit; tomatoes; milk	White Fish Pasta Bake, small pieces of carrot; Quick Summer Surprise	Creamy Ham & Peas with Penne; cheese; fruit salad	MILK

White Fish Pasta Bake

Serves 4   This fish pie is topped with pasta and mozzarella cheese rather than creamed potato.

6 oz/175 g dried penne or macaroni

2 tsp olive oil, plus extra for the pasta

2 eggs

2 small onions, very finely chopped

2 small celery stalks, very finely chopped

2 small carrots, peeled and very finely chopped

⅜ cup frozen peas

generous 1 cup milk

4 tbsp heavy cream

½ cup grated sharp Cheddar cheese

1 tsp Dijon mustard

good squeeze of fresh lemon juice

16 oz/455g white fish, skinned, boned, and sliced

6 oz/175 g mozzarella cheese, sliced

Preheat the oven to 400°F/200°C. Cook the pasta in a large pan of boiling water according to the package directions, then drain well. Return to the pan, then add a little oil and toss to coat.

Bring a small pan of water to a boil and add the eggs. Cook for 8–10 minutes, or until the eggs are hard cooked. Cool the eggs under cold running water.

Heat the oil in a heavy-bottom skillet and cook the onions, stirring occasionally, for 8 minutes, or until softened. Add the celery and carrots and cook for 3 minutes. Add the peas and cook for 2 minutes, or until tender. Stir in the milk and cream and bring to a boil. Turn off the heat and stir in the Cheddar cheese, mustard, and lemon juice.

Put the fish in a small, ovenproof dish. Shell and chop the eggs. Spoon over the fish, then top with the sauce. Arrange the pasta over the top and cover with the mozzarella cheese. Bake in the preheated oven for 20–25 minutes, or until brown on top.

Roast Vegetable Lasagna

Serves 4   This delicious lasagna is packed with different vegetables.

Preheat the oven to 375°F/190°C. **Put** the oil in a large bowl, add the zucchini, bell peppers, eggplant, onions, and shallots and **toss** well **to coat**.

Divide the vegetables between 2 baking sheets and roast in the preheated oven for 30–40 minutes until **soft** and **flecked** with brown. **Add** the white mushrooms after 20 minutes.

Remove the vegetables from the oven and tip into a large bowl. **Add** the tomatoes and tomato paste and **mix** well.

Melt the butter in a pan over low heat. **Stir** in the flour and cook, stirring constantly, for 2–3 minutes. Gradually **add** the milk and cook, continuing to stir constantly, until the sauce is thick and smooth. **Season** to taste with salt and pepper and **stir** in the Cheddar.

Layer the vegetable mixture and sauce in an ovenproof dish with the lasagna, finishing with a layer of sauce. **Sprinkle** over the Parmesan cheese and **bake** in the oven for 30–35 minutes. **Remove** from the oven and **serve** hot with a green salad.

3 tbsp olive oil

4 zucchini, halved lengthwise
    and thickly sliced

3 red bell peppers, seeded and chopped

1 eggplant, chopped

2 red onions, chopped

5 shallots, peeled and quartered

9 oz/250 g white mushrooms

14 oz/400 g canned chopped tomatoes

1 tbsp tomato paste

3½ tbsp butter

generous ⅓ cup all-purpose flour or
    gluten-free flour

2½ cups whole milk

3½ oz/100 g Cheddar cheese, grated

7 oz/200 g fresh lasagna noodles

2 tbsp grated Parmesan cheese

sea salt and pepper

salad greens, to serve

Rösti Nests

Serves 4   These always go down well with kids and if cut into wedges they can be eaten with the fingers. An egg nestles in the center of each rösti.

1 lb 5 oz/600 g potatoes such as Russet, unpeeled and halved

2 large carrots, each cut into 3 chunks

2 tbsp olive oil, plus extra for oiling and brushing

4 eggs

steamed fine green beans, to serve

These rösti can be made the day before without the egg and stored in the refrigerator, layered between sheets of parchment paper. Simply cook when required.

Steam the potatoes for 10 minutes, or until just tender. **Add** the carrots 5 minutes before the end of the cooking time. **Leave** the vegetables to cool, then **peel** the potatoes. Coarsely **grate** the potatoes and carrots into a bowl.

Loosely **form** the mixture into 4 circles so that the edges are fairly ragged, and **make** a well in the center—they are quite fragile, so handle with care.

Preheat the broiler to medium and oil 2 baking sheets. **Put** 2 rösti on each of the prepared baking sheets and **brush** the tops with more oil. **Cook** under the broiler, in 2 batches, for 7 minutes on one side, then **turn** over and cook on the other side for 5 minutes. **Keep** the cooked rösti warm while cooking the remaining rösti.

Break an egg into the well in the center of each rösti and **broil** for an additional 4 minutes, or until the rösti are golden and the egg is set. **Serve** with steamed fine green beans.

Ground Beef with Apricots

Serves 4   This Moroccan-inspired dish does not contain any spice, although adults may like to up the amount by adding a teaspoonful of chili powder, coriander, or cumin. Red meat is a valuable sauce of iron, which is further enhanced by the dried fruit. Serve with rice or in a tortilla wrap.

2 tbsp olive oil

1 onion, very finely chopped

scant 2 cups fresh lean ground beef

2 garlic cloves, very finely chopped

1 bay leaf

6–8 no-soak, unsulfured dried apricots, chopped

1¾ cups strained canned tomatoes

1 tbsp tomato paste

5½ oz/150 g canned no-salt, no-sugar cranberry beans, drained and rinsed

scant 1 cup vegetable stock

Heat the oil in a large pan or skillet and **cook** the onion, **stirring** for 8 minutes, or until softened and slightly golden.

Add the ground beef and cook, **breaking** it up with a spatula, for 4 minutes, or until browned. **Stir** in the garlic, spices, if using, and bay leaf and **cook**, stirring, for an additional minute.

Add the apricots, strained tomatoes, tomato paste, beans, and stock and **cook**, partially covered and **stirring** occasionally, for 25–30 minutes, or until the sauce has reduced and thickened. **Remove** the lid if the sauce looks too watery. Remove from the heat and discard the bay leaf, then serve.

Salmon Fish Cakes

Serves 4 Fresh salmon is used to make these fish cakes, but canned salmon speeds up their preparation slightly and makes a convenient alternative, although it is not as rich in the brain-boosting omega-3 fatty acids.

12 oz/350 g salmon fillets, skinned
  and boned
milk, for poaching
1 lb 7 oz/650 g potatoes, peeled and
  cut into chunks
1 tbsp tomato ketchup

2 tsp Dijon mustard
2 scallions, finely sliced
all-purpose flour, for dusting
corn or sunflower-seed oil, for pan-frying
salt and pepper

Put the salmon in a large, shallow pan and just cover with milk. Bring to a boil, then reduce the heat and let simmer for 3–4 minutes, or until just cooked. Lift out the fish from the pan and reserve the poaching milk. Let the salmon cool slightly, then flake the flesh into large chunks, removing any stray bones.

Meanwhile, boil the potatoes in a large pan of water for 15 minutes, or until tender. Drain, then return to the pan and mash with 2–3 tablespoons of the reserved poaching milk—you need a dry but lump-free mash.

Stir the ketchup, mustard, scallions, and half the salmon into the creamed potatoes. Season to taste with salt and pepper. Mix until well combined, then add the remaining salmon to the potato mixture, mixing gently to avoid breaking up the pieces of fish.

Dust a large plate and your hands with flour and shape the mixture into 8 cakes, then lightly coat each cake in the flour. Put the fish cakes on a cookie sheet and cover with plastic wrap, then refrigerate for 30 minutes to firm up.

Heat enough oil to cover the bottom of a large skillet generously. Cook the fish cakes, in batches, for 3 minutes on each side, or until crisp and golden. Keep the cooked fish cakes warm while cooking the remainder. Cut up into small pieces or mash for your child, depending on his or her age.

Creamy Ham & Peas with Penne

Serves 4   This simple dish always goes down well. Boost its nutrient content further by serving it with steamed broccoli.

10 oz/280 g dried penne

2 tbsp olive oil

1 onion, very finely chopped

1 tsp dried oregano

2 garlic cloves, very finely chopped

generous 1 cup vegetable or chicken stock

1³/₈ cups frozen baby peas

4 slices good-quality ham, cut into
   small pieces

6 tbsp sour cream

pepper (optional)

freshly grated Parmesan cheese, to serve

Cook the pasta in a large pan of boiling water according to the package directions. Drain, reserving 2 tablespoons of the cooking water. Meanwhile, heat the oil in a heavy-bottom skillet and cook the onion, stirring occasionally, for 8 minutes, or until soft and slightly golden. Add the oregano and garlic and cook, stirring, for 1 minute.

Add the stock and bring to a boil, then reduce the heat and let simmer for 2 minutes.

Stir in the baby peas, ham, and sour cream and cook over low heat, stirring frequently, until warmed through. Stir in the pasta and the reserved cooking water, then season to taste with pepper, if desired. Cut up the pasta and mash the peas and serve sprinkled with Parmesan cheese.

Canned, drained tuna, sautéed mushrooms, or cooked chicken are equally delicious in this sauce, but if using fish, omit the Parmesan cheese.

Quick Summer Surprise

Serves 4   This dessert should be left overnight, but this version takes a fraction of the time to prepare and tastes just as good. Use decorative pastry cutters to form the bread into fun shapes, but make sure they are the same size as the bread slices, because small shapes will end up as a soggy mess.

2 lb/900 g fresh mixed berries and currants, such as strawberries, raspberries, blackberries, and black currants, hulled (and the large fruit sliced)

scant $2/3$–generous $3/4$ cup superfine sugar, according to taste

$2/3$ cup water

8 slices day-old white bread, crusts removed

Put the fruit in a pan with the sugar and water. **Bring** to a boil, then reduce the heat and let **simmer** for 5 minutes, or until the fruit is soft and juicy.

Cut the bread into your chosen shape(s)—make sure that you have 2 of each shape—using a large pastry cutter. (The cutter should use as much of the bread slice as possible to avoid wastage.)

Arrange half the bread shapes in a shallow dish, then spoon over most of the warm fruit. **Put** the remaining bread shapes on top of the fruit and bread, then **spoon** over the warm juice. **Press** down lightly to enable the syrup to soak into the bread. **Let stand** for about 30 minutes before serving, topped with the remaining fruit.

If your toddler dislikes seeds or finding tiny pieces of fruit in fruit purée, strain the fruit before spooning it over the bread.

Fruitybocker Glory

Serves 4   This healthy twist on the kid's classic ice-cream sundae is sure to become a firm favorite.

1 large mango, seeded, peeled, and
   coarsely chopped
1 tbsp chopped mixed nuts or slivered
   almonds (optional)
4–8 scoops good-quality vanilla ice cream
handful of chopped strawberries,
   to decorate
4 teddy-shaped cookies, to serve (optional)

Put the mango flesh in a blender or food processor and process until blended and smooth. Press through a strainer to remove any fibers from the mangoes.

Lightly toast the nuts, if using, in a dry skillet. Let cool.

To serve, place a few spoonfuls of the mango in each of 4 sundae glasses. Top with 1–2 scoops of ice cream, depending on your child's age. Spoon over more mango sauce, then decorate with the strawberries and nuts, and serve with the cookies, if using.

Instead of mango, try strawberry, peach, or nectarine purée.

Strawberry Yogurt Pops

Serves 4   Strawberries have been used here because they are universally popular with children, but other types of fruit are also popular. The pops are basically a frozen smoothie, so they can also be served unfrozen.

2³/₈ cups fresh strawberries, hulled
   and sliced
generous 1¹/₄ cups thick plain yogurt
3 tbsp runny honey
few drops of vanilla extract

Put all in the ingredients in a blender or food processor and process until smooth.

Pour the mixture into ice-pop molds and freeze until solid—fun-shaped molds are popular with children.

Most types of soft fruit can be used to make frozen pops.
Try raspberries, mangoes, peaches, nectarines, plums, or oranges, or try a combination. You can also use just fruit and exclude the yogurt, if preferred. (Do not give honey to babies under one year.)

61

18–36 months

There is a world of difference between an 18-month and a 3-year-old child, in terms of both behavior and development. Yet similarities do exist—toddlers between these ages generally have a strong desire to feed themselves, and can be fussy eaters at times.

Variety and balance are the key to good health and by this age your toddler should be eating a wider range of foods and enjoying similar meals to the rest of the family.

Meal Planner

18 to 24 months: chopped foods.

24 to 36 months: cut-up foods.

Drinks: breast, cow's milk (or other alternatives), water, diluted, unsweetened fruit juice, smoothies.

Suitable foods: same as rest of family.

Avoid: raw eggs, whole nuts, salt, and overly spicy food.

	BREAKFAST	LUNCH	DINNER	BEDTIME
DAY 1	Apricot Oatmeal, chopped banana; toast; milk	Salmon Fish Cakes, homemade fries, peas, broccoli; yogurt	Simple Tomato Gnocchi; sugar snap peas; Baked Peach Crumbles	MILK
DAY 2	Boiled egg and slices of toast with yeast extract; fruit; milk	Rösti Nests, vegetables; crackers & cheese	Creamy Ham & Pea with Penne; broccoli; Strawberry Yogurt Pops	MILK
DAY 3	Low- or no-sugar cereal; banana bread; milk	Nectarine, Ham & Cheese Salad, spiral pasta; Mango & Yogurt Purée	Mini Burgers; diced vegetables; banana slices; cinnamon toast	MILK
DAY 4	Apricot Oatmeal, sliced banana; toast; milk	Baked potato, chickpea dip, cheese, diced carrot; yogurt & fruit	Pork & Apple Pan-Fry; diced potatoes & vegetables; Fruit Sherbet	MILK
DAY 5	Cereal & raisins; toast; fruit juice	Starfish Casserole, broccoli, peas; Honeycomb Ice Cream	White Fish Pasta Bake; diced vegetables; oat-style cookies & yogurt	MILK
DAY 6	Crêpes with fruit filling; yogurt; milk	Ground Beef with Apricots, pasta; Melon Fruit Bowl	Potato Pancakes with Bacon; grated carrot; Fruitybocker Glory	MILK
DAY 7	Poached egg, broiled tomatoes; toast; yogurt; fruit juice	Grilled chicken breast, diced vegetables; Quick Summer Surprise	Salmon & Broccoli Pasta; broiled tomatoes; Apple & Plum Yogurt	MILK

Pork & Apple Pan-Fry

Serves 4   The apple adds a delicious sweetness and texture to this one-pan meal. It is a big hit served with a dollop of creamed potato or rice.

1 tbsp all-purpose flour

15 oz/425 g pork tenderloin, trimmed and cut into bite-size pieces

2 tbsp olive oil

1 onion, very finely chopped

2 garlic cloves, chopped

1 tbsp very finely chopped fresh rosemary

1 large carrot, peeled and very finely chopped

2 dessert apples, peeled, cored, and chopped

generous 1 cup vegetable stock

3 tbsp sour cream

salt and pepper

Put the flour in a small plastic food bag and add salt and pepper to taste, then add the pork. Shake the bag to coat the pork in the seasoned flour. Turn the pork out onto a plate and shake off any excess flour.

Heat the oil in a large, heavy-bottom skillet and cook the pork, turning frequently, for 5 minutes, or until sealed and browned all over. Add the onion and garlic and cook, stirring occasionally, until softened.

Mix in the rosemary, carrot, and apples, then cook for 4 minutes, or until the apples begin to break down.

Pour in the stock and bring to a boil, then reduce the heat and let simmer, partially covered, for 15–20 minutes, or until reduced and thickened. Stir in the sour cream and heat through before serving.

Salmon & Broccoli Pasta

Serves 2   This healthy dish provides a delicious combination of cream cheese, salmon, broccoli, and pasta.

Cook the pasta in a pan of boiling water according to the package directions, then drain. Steam the broccoli for 7–10 minutes, or until tender.

Meanwhile, prepare the sauce. Melt the butter with the oil in a small, heavy-bottom skillet and cook the onion, stirring occasionally, for 8 minutes, or until softened. Add the salmon and cook for 2 minutes, or until just cooked and opaque. Stir in the cream cheese and milk and heat through.

Combine the sauce with the pasta and broccoli. Chop or mash the mixture.

3 oz/85 g dried small pasta shells

2 oz/55 g broccoli florets

small piece of unsalted butter

1 tsp olive oil

1 small onion, very finely chopped

5 oz/140 g wild or organic salmon fillet, skinned and boned, cubed

4 tbsp garlic-and-herb or plain cream cheese

2–3 tbsp whole milk

Starfish Casserole

Serves 4   Golden puff-pastry shapes add a fun element to this creamy fish casserole, but you can opt for creamed potato if preferred. It is wise to sift through the casserole with a fork before serving to check for any stray bones.

2 tbsp olive oil

1 large onion, very finely chopped

2 celery stalks

1 carrot, peeled and very finely chopped

large handful of spinach leaves, tough
   stalks removed, finely shredded

1 tbsp cornstarch

1¾ cups whole milk

4 tbsp cream cheese

½ cup grated mature Cheddar cheese

1 tsp Dijon mustard

good squeeze of fresh lemon juice

18 oz/500 g white fish, skinned and
   boned, cut into pieces

2 hard-cooked eggs

1 sheet of ready-rolled puff pastry,
   thawed if frozen

all-purpose flour, for dusting

1 egg, beaten, to glaze

salt and pepper

Preheat the oven to 400°F/200°C.

Heat the oil in a heavy-bottom skillet and cook the onion, stirring occasionally, for 8 minutes, or until softened. Add the celery and carrot and cook for 3 minutes. Add the shredded spinach and cook for 2 minutes, or until tender.

Stir in the cornstarch, milk, and cream cheese and bring to a boil. Turn off the heat and stir in the cheese, mustard, and lemon juice. Season to taste with salt and pepper.

Put the fish in an ovenproof dish. Shell and chop the eggs, then spoon over the fish. Top with the sauce.

Lay the pastry out on a lightly floured counter. Cut out fish and starfish shapes using pastry cutters, then arrange them on top of the casserole. Brush the pastry shapes with beaten egg.

Bake the casserole in the preheated oven for 20–25 minutes, or until the fish is cooked and the pastry shapes have risen and are a golden brown color.

Nectarine, Ham & Cheese Salad

Serves 4   This salad is a healthy combination of fruit, vegetables, and protein-rich foods. It's a good idea to serve the salad dressing separately, because some children prefer their salad "nude." It's also one of those salads that younger children who have not yet mastered using a fork can eat with their fingers.

12 baby new potatoes, scrubbed and halved

4 large romaine lettuce leaves

3 nectarines, pitted and cubed

2 thick slices good-quality ham, any fat removed, cut into cubes

3 thick slices Cheddar cheese, diced

12 cherry tomatoes, halved

dressing

2 tbsp store-bought mayonnaise

1 tbsp extra-virgin olive oil

1 tsp lemon juice

Beat the dressing ingredients together in a small bowl.

Cook the potatoes in a pan of boiling water for 10 minutes, or until tender. **Drain** and set aside.

Place a lettuce leaf in the base of each of 4 serving bowls. **Divide** the potatoes, nectarines, ham, cheese, and tomatoes between each bowl. **Serve** the salad with the dressing.

Potato Pancakes with Bacon

Serves 4   If you are stuck for breakfast ideas, these pancakes are an excellent way of using up leftover creamed potatoes. They are also great for a quick tea served with baked beans and sausages.

4½ oz/125 g cold, creamed potatoes

1 cup milk

scant ¾ cup self-rising flour

1 large egg, beaten

corn or sunflower-seed oil, for pan-frying

to serve

broiled, good-quality bacon

broiled halved tomatoes

Put the creamed potatoes and milk in a blender or food processor and process to a thin purée.

Put the flour in a bowl and make a well in the center. Add the egg and potato purée to the well and gradually beat in the flour to make a fairly thick, smooth batter.

Heat a little oil in a large, heavy-bottom skillet. Place one small ladleful of batter per potato pancake into the skillet—you will need to cook them in batches. Cook the potato pancakes for 2 minutes on each side, or until golden. Keep the cooked potato pancakes warm while cooking the remaining pancakes.

Divide the potato pancakes between 4 serving plates and serve with the bacon and tomatoes.

Simple Tomato Gnocchi

Serves 4   Gnocchi is perfect comfort food and takes just over a minute to cook. Here, it comes with a simple tomato sauce with added vegetables, although you would never know because the sauce is puréed until smooth. The sugar removes the slight sharpness of the tomatoes, but it can be left out.

2 tbsp olive oil

1 garlic clove, chopped

1 tsp dried oregano

1 carrot, grated

1 small red bell pepper, seeded and
very finely chopped

2½ cups strained canned tomatoes

5 tbsp water or stock

1 tbsp tomato paste

½ tsp sugar

1 lb 2 oz/500 g gnocchi

freshly grated Parmesan cheese, to serve

Heat the oil in a heavy-bottom skillet and **cook** the garlic and oregano, stirring, for 1 minute. **Add** the carrot and red bell pepper and cook over medium-low heat, stirring frequently, for 4 minutes, or until softened.

Pour in the strained canned tomatoes and water and stir in the tomato paste and sugar. Partially **cover** and cook, stirring occasionally, for 15 minutes, or until reduced and thickened.

Transfer the mixture to a blender or food processor and process until blended and smooth. **Return** to the pan and reheat. **Add** a little more water if the sauce appears dry.

Meanwhile, **cook** the gnocchi in a large pan of boiling water according to the package directions. **Drain** and gently mix into the sauce, taking care not to break up the gnocchi.

Divide the gnocchi between 4 shallow bowls and serve sprinkled with Parmesan cheese.

For a variation, try stirring cooked split lentils into the tomato sauce instead of vegetables, then process the sauce until smooth.

Mini Burgers

Serves 4   There's something very appealing about bite-size foods and these mini burgers are no exception, fitting perfectly into those baby sesame or poppy seed buns you can now buy. These burgers are perfect for little hands to hold and are easy to eat.

¾ cup fresh whole-wheat bread crumbs

1 tsp dried oregano

1 onion, grated

1 carrot, peeled and grated

1 garlic clove, crushed

scant 2 cups fresh, lean ground beef

1 tbsp tomato paste

1 egg, beaten

vegetable oil, for pan-frying

salt and pepper

to serve

mini burger buns

tomato slices

lettuce leaves

ketchup or relish of choice

Put all the burger ingredients, except the oil, in a large bowl and mix together with your hands until combined. Shape the mixture into small balls. Cover with plastic wrap, and refrigerate for 15 minutes.

Heat enough oil to cover the bottom of a large, heavy-bottom skillet and cook the burgers for 3–5 minutes, turning halfway, until cooked through and browned all over.

Serve each burger in a mini burger bun with tomato and lettuce, and ketchup or relish.

Baked Peach Crumbles

Serves 4   These crumbles are especially good with a dollop of yogurt or ice cream. Apples, plums, and nectarines also work well.

4 peaches, halved and pitted

scant ⅓ cup all-purpose flour, sifted

2 tbsp unsalted butter, diced, plus extra
   for greasing

2 tbsp instant oatmeal

3 tbsp brown sugar

Try adding 1 tablespoon finely chopped nuts and 1 tablespoon very finely chopped dried dates to the crumble mixture.

Preheat the oven to 350°F/180°C. **Arrange** the peach halves in the bottom of a small, lightly greased, ovenproof dish.

Put the flour in a bowl, then add the butter and rub in with your fingertips until coarse bread crumbs form. **Stir** in the oatmeal and sugar and **mix** well.

Sprinkle generous amounts of the crumble mixture over the peach halves. **Bake** in the preheated oven for 25–30 minutes, or until the peaches are tender and the crumble is slightly crisp and golden.

Honeycomb Ice Cream

Serves 8   This light, vanilla ice cream is flecked with pieces of honeycomb. An ice-cream maker is not essential—it is equally good made by hand.

1¾ cups heavy cream

1¼ cups thick plain yogurt

1 tsp vanilla extract

4 tbsp honey

4 tbsp maple syrup

3 honeycomb chocolate bars, broken into small chunks

Honey is not recommended for children under one year old, due to its high sugar content and slight risk of food poisoning.

Whisk the cream in a large bowl until thickened, then **fold** in the yogurt followed by the vanilla extract, honey, and maple syrup.

Pour the mixture into a 2-quart freezerproof container with a lid and freeze for 2 hours. **Remove** from the freezer and beat with a whisk or fork to break up the ice crystals. **Stir** in the honeycomb, then return to the freezer and freeze for an additional 2 hours. **Beat** again, as before, and return to the freezer.

Repeat this process twice more, then freeze until solid.

Remove from the freezer 45 minutes before serving to let the ice cream soften.

Melon Fruit Bowl

Serves 4 If your child needs extra encouragement to eat fruit, then this attractive fruit-filled melon is bound to appeal. Make the fruit salad just before serving to retain as much of the fruit's nutrients as possible.

½ large Galia, Charentais, or Cantaloupe
   melon, seeded
a selection of fresh fruit depending on
   what's in season and popular, such as
   strawberries, raspberries, blueberries,
   orange segments, seedless grapes, slices of
   peach or nectarine, and chunks of banana
2 tbsp fresh orange juice

Cut a sliver off the base of the melon half so that it stands upright and place on a serving plate.

Cut the top off the melon and scoop out most of the flesh using a melon baller or teaspoon to leave a hollow bowl shape.

Put the melon balls and the remaining fruit in a large bowl and pour over the orange juice. Turn to coat the fruit in the juice, then spoon the fruit into the melon shell. Pour over any remaining juice.

3–4 years

Your child will by now be happily practicing his or her eating skills, which can be a messy affair but is nevertheless a crucial stage in a child's development. Accept and be prepared for the mess and try to resist the temptation to intervene too much. Alongside developing his or her own individuality, your three- to four-year-old will also become increasingly affected by outside influences, especially if he or she attends a playgroup or pre-school. These factors can all play a part in determining his or her food preferences.

Meal Planner

Three- to four-year-olds are generally very active and their diets need to allow for this increase in energy levels. Variety and balance are vital dietary considerations.

Avoid: whole nuts.

	BREAKFAST	LUNCH	DINNER	BEDTIME
DAY 1	Cereal; toast; melon; fruit juice	Bacon, Pea & Potato Frittata; Flower Power Salad; yogurt	Chicken Fajitas with Guacamole, cherry tomatoes; Mini Muffins with Toffee Sauce	MILK
DAY 2	Cereal; croissant; Peach Melba Smoothie	Baked potato, tuna & corn kernels; baked apple & yogurt	Salmon Fish Cakes, potato wedges, broccoli, peas; Quick Summer Surprise	MILK
DAY 3	Poached egg; Apricot Oatmeal; toast; fruit juice	Creamy Ham & Pea with Penne, broccoli; fruit salad	Winter Sausage Casserole, creamed potatoes, vegetables; Baked Peach Crumbles	MILK
DAY 4	Cereal; toast; fruit juice	Creamy Tomato & Lentil Soup, lightly toasted bagel; Banana & Vanilla Malt	Golden Fish Fingers with Sweet Potato Wedges, peas; Yogurt & Mango Purée	MILK
DAY 5	Potato Pancakes with Bacon; Peach Melba Smoothie	Pesto-Topped Cod, potatoes, vegetables; Double Banana Crêpes	Falafel Burgers, diced vegetables, chickpea dip; Fruitybocker Glory	MILK
DAY 6	Scrambled egg; toast; tomatoes; Super Juice	Pork Fricassee, rice, vegetables; Melon Fruit Bowl	Broiled chicken breast, salad, new potatoes; fruit	MILK
DAY 7	Apricot Oatmeal; fruit; toast; fruit juice	Salmon & Broccoli Pasta, vegetables; yogurt & fruit	Tofu & Vegetable Stir-Fry, cottage cheese; Honeycomb Ice Cream	MILK

Golden Fish Fingers with Sweet Potato Wedges

Serves 4   If making your own fish fingers sounds like too much effort, this simple version may change your mind, and you can also guarantee the quality of the ingredients used. The white fish fillets are covered in a crisp, golden crumb, made from fresh bread crumbs, and served with sweet potato wedges.

10 oz/280 g thick white fish fillets, skinned
  and boned
all-purpose flour, for dusting
1 tsp paprika
1 egg, beaten
fresh bread crumbs or fine cornmeal,
  for coating
corn or sunflower-seed oil, for pan-frying

salt and pepper
freshly cooked peas, to serve

sweet potato wedges
1 lb/450 g sweet potatoes, scrubbed and
  cut into wedges
1 tbsp olive oil

Preheat the oven to 400°F/200°C.

Dry the sweet potato wedges on a clean dish towel. Put the oil in a roasting pan and heat for a few minutes in the preheated oven. Arrange the potatoes in the pan and bake for 30–35 minutes, turning them halfway through the cooking time, until they are tender and golden.

Meanwhile, cut the white fish into strips about ¾ inch/2 cm wide.

Season the flour to taste with salt and pepper and add the paprika. Roll the white fish strips in the seasoned flour until coated, shaking off any excess, then dip them in the beaten egg. Roll the strips in the bread crumbs until evenly coated.

Heat enough oil to cover the bottom of a large, nonstick skillet. Carefully arrange the fish fingers in the skillet—you may need to cook them in batches—and cook for 3–4 minutes on each side, or until crisp and golden. Drain on paper towels before serving, if necessary.

Serve the fish fingers with the sweet potato wedges, and some freshly cooked peas.

Bacon, Pea & Potato Frittata

Serves 4   This frittata is similar to the Spanish tortilla. Serve it cut into wedges or slices, with crusty bread and green vegetable sticks or a salad. This is a good food for small fingers to handle.

2–3 slices good-quality bacon

1½ tbsp olive oil

1 onion, very finely chopped

12 oz/350 g new potatoes, cooked, and
   halved or quartered, if large

½ cup frozen baby peas

6 eggs, lightly beaten

salt and pepper

tomato wedges, to serve

Canned, drained tuna; cooked leeks; frozen or canned, drained corn kernels; ham; halved cherry tomatoes, or cubes of cheese are suitable alternatives to the ingredients used here.

Preheat the broiler to high. Cook the bacon under the broiler until crisp. Let cool slightly, then cut into small pieces and set aside.

Heat the oil in a large, heavy-bottom skillet with a heatproof handle and cook the onion, stirring occasionally, for 8 minutes, or until softened.

Add the potatoes and cook, turning frequently to prevent them sticking to the skillet, for 5 minutes, or until golden. Add the bacon and baby peas, then spread the mixture evenly over the bottom of the skillet.

Reheat the broiler to high. Lightly season the eggs with salt and pepper, then pour carefully over the onion and potato mixture. Cook over medium heat for 5–6 minutes, or until the eggs are just set and the base of the frittata is lightly golden brown.

Place the skillet under the broiler and cook the top for 3 minutes, or until set and lightly golden. Serve the frittata warm or cold, cut into wedges or slices, with fresh tomato wedges.

Winter Sausage Casserole

Serves 4   This casserole has a biscuit topping and can be made with either pork or vegetarian sausages.

6 good-quality pork or vegetarian sausages

1 tbsp olive oil

1 onion, chopped

1 garlic clove, chopped

1 celery stalk, very finely chopped

1 red bell pepper, seeded and diced

2 zucchini, diced

2 tsp chopped fresh rosemary

1 tsp dried thyme

1 bay leaf

1¼ cups vegetable stock

1¼ cups strained canned tomatoes

½ tsp sugar

14 oz/400 g canned cranberry beans, drained and rinsed

biscuit topping

scant 1¼ cups self-rising flour, sifted, plus extra for dusting

½ tsp salt

1 heaping tsp baking powder

3 tbsp butter or margarine, cut into small pieces

about ¼–⅓ cup milk

Preheat the broiler to medium-high. Line the broiler pan with foil. **Arrange** the sausages on the broiler rack and cook under the broiler, turning frequently, until cooked through and golden all over. Set aside.

Preheat the oven to 400°F/200°C. Meanwhile, **heat** the oil in a heavy-bottom skillet and **cook** the onion, covered, for 5 minutes, or until softened. **Add** the garlic, celery, red bell pepper, zucchini, rosemary, thyme, and the bay leaf and cook, covered, for 5 minutes.

Add the vegetable stock and cook over medium-high heat for a few minutes. **Reduce** the heat to medium and **stir**, then add the strained canned tomatoes and sugar. **Stir** again and cook for 10 minutes, or until the sauce has reduced and begins to thicken.

Slice the sausages and **add** to the sauce with the beans. **Stir** and **spoon** the mixture into a casserole dish.

To make the biscuit topping, **put** the flour, salt, and baking powder in a bowl and **mix** together. **Add** the butter and **rub** in with your fingertips until bread crumbs form.

Gradually **stir** in the milk using a spatula, adding just enough to bring the mixture together. Form into a dough with floured hands. **Knead** lightly on a floured counter until smooth. **Take** walnut-size pieces of the dough and roll into balls. **Flatten** and arrange in a circle on top of the casserole. **Brush** the top of the biscuits with the remaining or extra milk.

Bake the dish in the preheated oven for 20 minutes, or until the biscuits are risen and golden.

Pork Fricassee

Serves 4   If you are looking for a quick alternative to a roast, this creamy pork dish may be just the answer. Serve it with rice or boiled new potatoes and green vegetables.

2 tbsp all-purpose flour

4 lean pork tenderloin, about 5 oz/140 g
   each, cut into bite-size pieces

about 1 tbsp olive oil

1 onion, very finely chopped

1¼ cups chicken stock

2 garlic cloves, chopped

1 red bell pepper, seeded and diced

1–2 tsp dried thyme

6 tbsp canned no-salt, no-sugar corn
   kernels, drained and rinsed

4–6 tbsp sour cream

salt and pepper

Put the flour in a bowl and season to taste with salt and pepper. **Toss** the pieces of pork in the seasoned flour.

Heat the oil in a large, heavy-bottom skillet with a lid. Cook the onion, **stirring** occasionally, for 8 minutes, or until softened and slightly golden. **Remove** with a slotted spoon and set aside. **Add** the pork and more oil if necessary and cook, turning frequently, for 5 minutes, or until sealed and browned all over. **Add** a little of the stock if the meat begins to stick. **Return** the onion to the pan with the garlic, bell pepper, and thyme and **cook**, **stirring**, for another 3 minutes. **Add** the corn, then increase the heat and **boil** until the liquid has reduced.

Reduce the heat and stir in the stock. Cover and cook for 10 minutes. **Stir** in the sour cream and warm through.

Chicken or turkey can be used instead of pork.

Flower Power Salad

Serves 4   Few parents or carers are into spending hours turning meals into pretty pictures, but occasionally it's fun to experiment, and when it comes to encouraging children to eat fruit and vegetables, every little helps. Children can also get involved in making these individual "flower-shaped" salads.

2¾-inch/7-cm piece cucumber, diced

4 baby corn, blanched and cut
   into circles

1 carrot, diced

12 black, seedless grapes, halved

2 large tomatoes, halved and seeded

1 tbsp sunflower seeds, toasted

4 fine green beans, steamed

8 snow peas, steamed

dressing

2 tbsp extra-virgin olive oil

1 tsp white wine vinegar

1 tsp store-bought mayonnaise

Whisk all the dressing ingredients together in a pitcher.

Put the cucumber, baby corn, carrot, and grapes in a bowl and pour over enough dressing to coat the salad.

Spoon an equal quantity of the salad into each tomato half, then arrange on serving plates. Sprinkle the tops with the sunflower seeds. Put a green bean under each tomato to represent a flower stem and arrange the snow peas as leaves.

Pesto-Topped Cod

Serves 4   Encouraging children to eat fish can be difficult—the crumb-coated variety being the exception. In this recipe, a spoonful of pesto and slices of mozzarella mask any fishiness.

4 thick cod fillets, about
  5½ oz/150 g each

olive oil, for brushing

4 tbsp ready-made red pesto

2 tomatoes, seeded and sliced

8 slices mozzarella cheese

Preheat the broiler to high and line the broiler pan with foil. Brush each piece of cod with a little oil. Arrange the fish in the broiler pan and cook under the broiler for 2 minutes on one side, then turn over and cook on the other side for 2 minutes, or until the fish is opaque.

Remove from the broiler and spread a tablespoon of pesto over each fillet. Arrange the tomato slices on top, then the cheese. Cook under the broiler for an additional 3 minutes, or until the cheese has melted and the fish is cooked through.

Fish is a good source of lowfat protein. Although white fish is not as rich in omega-3 fatty acids as oily fish, it still contains beneficial amounts.

Chicken Fajitas with Guacamole

Serves 4   Add a touch of Mexico to teatime with these wraps. Serve with carrot, cucumber, and celery sticks.

Mix the cumin, oil, garlic, and lime juice together in a nonmetallic shallow dish. Season the chicken to taste with salt and pepper, then add to the dish and turn to coat in the marinade. Cover with plastic wrap and let marinate in the refrigerator for up to 1 hour, turning the chicken occasionally.

To make the guacamole, mash the avocado, garlic, and lemon juice together in a bowl with a fork. Add the mayonnaise and salt and pepper to taste and mix until smooth and creamy. Set aside.

Preheat a stovetop grill pan. Remove the chicken from the marinade and brush with oil, then cook for 6–8 minutes, turning halfway through the cooking time, until cooked through and golden.

Meanwhile, warm the tortillas according to the package directions. Arrange an equal quantity of the chicken, red bell pepper, and scallions down the center of each. Add a spoonful of guacamole and roll up. Slice diagonally in half to serve.

1 tsp ground cumin

1 tbsp olive oil, plus extra for brushing

1 garlic clove, sliced

juice of 1 lime

4 chicken breasts, about 4 oz/115 g each, cut into strips

4 soft flour tortillas

1 red bell pepper, seeded and sliced

2 scallions, diagonally sliced

salt and pepper

guacamole

1 large avocado, pitted, and flesh scooped out and set aside

1 garlic clove, crushed

juice of ½ lemon

1 tbsp store-bought mayonnaise

Tofu & Vegetable Stir-Fry

Serves 4   Tofu is mildly flavored, but it is this quality that makes it so versatile. It readily absorbs stronger flavors such as those used here. Change the vegetables depending on what you have to hand. Serve with rice noodles.

10½ oz/300 g firm tofu (drained weight), patted dry and cut into cubes

2 tbsp corn or sunflower-seed oil, plus extra for oiling

9 oz/250 g broccoli, divided into florets and stems diagonally sliced

3½ oz/100 g fine green beans

1 carrot, cut into thin sticks

1 red bell pepper, seeded and sliced

3 scallions, diagonally sliced

5 tbsp orange juice

1 tbsp soy sauce, plus extra for serving (optional)

rice noodles, to serve

marinade

2 garlic cloves, finely sliced

1 tsp grated fresh gingerroot

6 tbsp black bean sauce

1 tbsp soy sauce

1 tbsp sesame oil

Mix the marinade ingredients together in a shallow dish. Add the tofu and turn to coat in the marinade. Cover with plastic wrap and marinate in the refrigerator for at least 1 hour, turning the tofu occasionally.

Meanwhile, preheat the oven to 375°F/190°C. Lightly oil a cookie sheet. Remove the tofu from the marinade, reserving the marinade, and spread out on the prepared cookie sheet. Roast in the preheated oven for 20–25 minutes, turning halfway through the cooking time, until golden and crisp.

Meanwhile, preheat a wok until hot. Add the oil and swirl it around the wok. Stir-fry the broccoli for 2 minutes, then toss in the beans, carrot, red bell pepper, and scallions and stir-fry for 2 minutes.

Pour in the orange juice and marinade and cook, stirring, until the liquid has reduced and thickened (add some water if the mixture appears too dry).

Serve the stir-fry with noodles, topped with the tofu. Serve with soy sauce, if desired.

Super Juice

Serves 4   Freshly made juices are an excellent way of boosting your child's intake of fruit and vegetables. Fresh juices should be diluted with water to reduce their strength and acidity and are best served straightaway.

4 dessert apples, cored and quartered

2 pears, cored and quartered

2 handfuls of black seedless grapes
   or black currants

Put the apples, pears, and grapes through a juicer. Dilute with water to taste and pour into 4 glasses.

Peach Melba Smoothie

Serves 4   The ice cream in this smoothie makes it taste very indulgent, but you could use plain yogurt instead for a healthier option. Vitamins and minerals as well as protein are found in beneficial amounts in this liquid version of the classic fruit dessert.

4 peaches or nectarines, peeled, pitted, and
   coarsely chopped

1½ cups raspberries

2½ cups milk

4 decent scoops of good-quality vanilla
   ice cream

Put all the ingredients in a blender or food processor and process until smooth and creamy.

Children aged 3–4 should have 4 glasses of fluids a day, which should be mainly water, but smoothies, milk, and diluted fresh fruit juices can also be included. Concentration and energy levels are detrimentally affected by dehydration.

Double Banana Crêpes

Makes 8   These crêpes are a perfect, child-friendly size and are so simple to make that children can get involved in their preparation—and flipping, if feeling brave! Serve topped with more banana and maple syrup.

Sift the flour, baking powder, and salt into a large bowl. Stir in the sugar. **Make** a well in the center.

Whisk the egg and milk together in a pitcher. Gradually **add** to the well, beating constantly and thoroughly to remove any lumps. **Let** stand for 30 minutes, to give the batter a lighter texture.

Stir in the mashed banana just before cooking. **Melt** half the butter in a large, heavy-bottom skillet over medium heat.

Ladle 3 separate spoonfuls of batter into the skillet (each crêpe is about 3¼ inches/ 8 cm in diameter) and **cook** for 2 minutes, or until the underside is golden. **Flip** the crêpe over with a spatula and cook on the other side for an additional 1–2 minutes.

Remove from the skillet and keep warm while you cook the remaining crêpes, adding the remaining butter as necessary.

Serve 2 crêpes per serving with sliced banana, a drizzle of maple syrup, and a dollop of yogurt.

scant 1¼ cups all-purpose flour

1 tsp baking powder

large pinch of salt

generous ⅛ cup unrefined superfine sugar

1 egg, beaten

scant 1 cup milk

1 large banana, mashed

2 tbsp unsalted butter

to serve

sliced banana

maple syrup

plain yogurt

Mini Muffins with Toffee Sauce

Makes 20   These muffins contain dates, which give them a moist texture. They're delicious on their own, but for a real treat, serve the muffins warm with the toffee sauce poured over.

1⅛ cups pitted dried dates, chopped

scant 1 cup water

1 tsp baking soda

4 tbsp unsalted butter

scant 1¼ cups self-rising flour

generous ¾ cup unrefined superfine sugar

1 tsp vanilla extract

2 eggs, beaten

toffee sauce

⅔ cup heavy cream

1 tbsp corn syrup

generous ⅓ cup packed brown sugar

4 tbsp unsalted butter

Preheat the oven to 350°F/180°C. Line two 12-hole muffin pans with 20 small paper cases.

Put the dates and water in a pan and bring to a boil. **Cook** over low heat for 10 minutes, or until softened. **Stir** in the baking soda and butter—it will froth up—and stir until the butter has melted.

Let cool slightly, then pour the mixture into a blender or food processor and process to a coarse purée.

Sift the flour into a large bowl and stir in the superfine sugar with a wooden spoon. **Add** the vanilla extract, eggs, and date purée

and mix until just combined. Don't overmix the batter, or the muffins will be heavy.

Divide the batter between the paper cases and bake in the preheated oven for 12–15 minutes, or until risen and golden brown. **Let** cool on a wire rack.

To make the sauce, **put** all the ingredients in a small pan. **Bring** to a boil, **stirring** constantly, then reduce the heat and let simmer for 10 minutes, or until thickened and glossy. **Remove** from the heat and let cool slightly.

Serve the muffins warm with the sauce poured over.

4 years plus

By this stage, your little one will have made the transition from toddler to young child, and with this comes an increasing independence and free spirit. He or she will start school in the near future and this presents its own challenges and changes.

It is important to enable your child's personality, sense of humor, and also their sense of self to flourish, without knocking his or her confidence if he or she sometimes goes awry. This is especially important at mealtimes, when guidance, gentle persuasion, and plenty of patience are vital if you are to avoid meals turning into a battleground.

Meal Planner

When planning meals, consider what you made the day before and possibly plan to serve the day after so you provide a good range of meals, encompassing a variety of ingredients. Your child will soon be starting school so a packed lunch may be an option.

Avoid: Whole nuts.

	BREAKFAST	LUNCH	DINNER
DAY 1	Cereal with chopped fruit; toast; fruit juice	Potato Pancakes with Bacon; Flower Power Salad; cream cheese & fruit; or packed or school lunch	Teriyaki Tuna with Vegetable Noodles; broccoli; Mini Muffins with Toffee Sauce
DAY 2	Boiled egg and slices of toast with yeast extract; fruit; Super Juice	Chicken Fajitas with Guacamole; vegetable sticks; fruit salad; or packed or school lunch	Green Giant Pasta; toasted bagel; salad; Strawberry Yogurt Pops
DAY 3	Cereal; toast; banana; fresh fruit juice	Honey Salmon Kabobs, grated carrot, new potatoes; yogurt; or packed or school lunch	Vegetable Egg Rolls with Dipping Sauce; noodles or rice; Honeycomb Ice Cream with chopped banana
DAY 4	Toasted ham & tomato sandwich; Peach Melba Smoothie	Creamy Tomato & Lentil Soup, bread; Fruit Sherbet; or packed or school lunch	Falafel Burgers, Sweet Potato Wedges; vegetable sticks; Baked Peach Crumbles
DAY 5	Breakfast Omelet; toast; melon; fruit juice	Chicken Fajitas with Guacamole; salad; Fresh Fruit Sticks; or packed or school lunch	Starfish Casserole; potatoes, vegetables; Double Chocolate Brownies; fresh fruit
DAY 6	Apricot Oatmeal; toast; Apple & Carrot Juice	Breakfast Omelet; French bread; vegetable sticks; yogurt	Winter Sausage Bake; creamed potatoes; vegetables; Fresh Fruit Sticks
DAY 7	Scrambled egg; tomatoes; Banana & Vanilla Malt	Broiled chicken breast, vegetables; Melon Fruit Bowl	Simple Tomato Gnocchi; broccoli; peas; Double Banana Crêpes

Breakfast Omelet

Serves 4 Despite the name, this substantial omelet can be served for lunch or dinner with a side order of vegetables and new potatoes.

4 good-quality pork or vegetarian sausages

small piece of butter

2 tsp corn oil, plus extra if necessary

12 cherry tomatoes

6 eggs, beaten

salt and pepper

Follow the same method to make a Spanish tortilla—omit the tomatoes and sausages and replace with cubes of cooked potato and sautéed onion slices.

Preheat the broiler to medium-high. Line the broiler pan with foil. Arrange the sausages on the broiler rack and cook under the broiler, turning frequently, until cooked through and golden all over. Let cool slightly, then cut into bite-size pieces.

Meanwhile, melt the butter with the oil in a medium-size skillet with a heatproof handle and cook the tomatoes, turning occasionally, for 2 minutes.

Add the sausage pieces so that they are evenly distributed in the bottom of the skillet among the tomatoes. Add a little more oil if the skillet appears dry.

Season the eggs to taste with salt and pepper and pour over the sausages and tomatoes. Cook for 3 minutes, without stirring, then place the skillet under the broiler and cook the top for 3 minutes, or until set and lightly golden. Cut into wedges to serve.

Vegetable Egg Rolls with Dipping Sauce

Makes 16   These bite-size egg rolls filled with stir-fried vegetables and noodles are popular with kids and adults alike. They are baked in the oven to keep fat levels down, but you can fry them instead if preferred.

1 tbsp corn or sunflower-seed oil, plus extra
   for oiling and brushing

2 oz/55 g dried vermicelli noodles

1 tsp toasted sesame oil

1 small red bell pepper, seeded and cut into
   thin strips

2 carrots, cut into thin strips

2 scallions, finely sliced lengthwise

2 oz/55 g baby corn, finely sliced

2 oz/55 g fine green beans, finely sliced

1-inch/2.5-cm piece fresh gingerroot, peeled
   and grated

1 tbsp soy sauce

⅜ cup bean sprouts

16 small egg roll skins, thawed
   if frozen

1 egg white, lightly beaten

dipping sauce

4 tbsp sweet plum sauce

3 tbsp store-bought mayonnaise

Preheat the oven to 350°F/180°C. Lightly oil a large cookie sheet. Prepare the noodles according to the package directions. Drain, then refresh under cold running water. Cut the noodles into short lengths with kitchen scissors and set aside.

Preheat a wok until hot. Add the oils and swirl around the wok. Stir-fry the red bell pepper, carrots, scallions, baby corn, and beans for 3 minutes. Add the ginger, soy sauce, and bean sprouts and stir-fry for 1 minute, or until the liquid evaporates.

Transfer the vegetables to a bowl with the noodles and mix until combined. Let cool.

Place an egg roll skin on a counter, keeping the remaining skins covered with a clean dish towel to prevent them drying out. **Place** a heaping tablespoon of the filling on the corner nearest to you, then fold the corner over the filling toward the center. **Fold** in the 2 sides of the skin to enclose the filling, then continue to roll. **Brush** the far corner with a little egg white and fold over to seal. **Repeat** with the remaining skins and filling to make 16 rolls—you may have a little of the filling left over.

Arrange the egg rolls on the prepared baking sheet and brush each one with oil. **Bake** in the preheated oven for 15–20 minutes, or until lightly golden and crisp on the outside.

Meanwhile, to make the dipping sauce, **mix** the plum sauce and mayonnaise together in a small bowl. **Serve** the egg rolls hot with the sauce.

Honey Salmon Kabobs

Serves 4   The marinade in this recipe gives a wonderful, sweet, caramel flavor and glossy coating to the fish. While kabobs are fun, do take care when giving them to children. If you use wooden skewers, soak them in water first to stop them burning.

4 boneless salmon fillets, each about
   5 oz/140 g, skinned and cut into
   ¾-inch/2-cm cubes
1 tbsp toasted sesame seeds (optional)
freshly cooked rice and peas, to serve

marinade

2 tbsp honey
2 tbsp soy sauce
1 tbsp olive oil
1 tsp toasted sesame oil

Mix the marinade ingredients together in a shallow dish. **Add** the salmon and stir to coat in the marinade. **Cover** with plastic wrap and let marinate in the refrigerator for 1 hour, turning the fish occasionally.

Preheat the broiler to high and line the broiler pan with foil. **Thread** the cubes of salmon onto 4–6 skewers. Arrange on the broiler rack and **brush** with the marinade. **Cook** under the broiler for 3–5 minutes, **turning** frequently, until cooked through.

Meanwhile, **put** the remaining marinade in a small pan and **heat** for a few minutes until it has reduced and thickened.

Serve the kabobs on a bed of rice and peas. **Spoon** the reduced marinade over the kabobs and **sprinkle** with the sesame seeds, if using.

Instead of the salmon, use cubes of firm white fish, fresh tuna, pork, beef, or chicken. Oily fish contains omega-3 fatty acids, which are essential for brain development, as well as healthy skin and eyes.

Falafel Burgers

Serves 4   Canned chickpeas are incredibly convenient and are a good source of iron, zinc, folate, and B vitamins.

14 oz/400 g canned no-salt, no-sugar
   chickpeas, drained and rinsed
1 onion, quartered
2 garlic cloves
1 tsp ground coriander
1 tsp ground cumin
1 slice whole-wheat bread, crusts removed,
   broken into pieces
1 egg, beaten

all-purpose flour, for dusting
2 tbsp corn oil, plus extra if necessary

To serve
4 seeded rolls or pita breads
tomato slices
lettuce leaves
chickpea dip, ketchup, or relish
   of choice

Any canned beans can be used in this recipe, although the firmer-textured ones such as kidney beans, cranberry, and cannellini work better. You could add chopped nuts and cooked lentils.

Put the chickpeas, onion, garlic, spices, and bread in a blender or food processor and **process** to a coarse paste. **Add** the egg and process again until combined. **Transfer** the mixture to a bowl. Cover with plastic wrap and chill for 1 hour to firm up.

Dust a plate and your hands with flour and **shape** the mixture into 4 burgers, then lightly coat each burger in flour.

Heat the oil in a large, heavy-bottom skillet. **Cook** the burgers, in batches and adding more oil if necessary, for 3 minutes on each side, or until golden. **Serve** the burgers in rolls or pita breads with tomato and lettuce, and chickpea dip or a relish.

Moroccan Chicken Couscous

Serves 2   This recipe may sound exotic, but it really is very easy to make and has just a hint of spice.

generous ¼ cup couscous

small piece of unsalted butter

3 tsp olive oil

1 small onion, very finely chopped

1 skinless chicken breast, cut into

   bite-size pieces

1 small garlic clove, very finely chopped

½ tsp ground cumin

pinch of ground coriander

1 small peach or nectarine, peeled, pitted,

   and diced

4 whole toasted almonds, very finely chopped

Put the couscous in a heatproof bowl and pour over boiling water until just covered. Cover and leave for 8–10 minutes, or until all the water has been absorbed, then mix in the butter and fluff up with a fork.

Meanwhile, heat half the oil in a heavy-bottom skillet and sauté the onion, stirring occasionally, for 8 minutes, or until softened. Add the remaining oil with the chicken and garlic and cook, stirring occasionally, for 5 minutes, or until the chicken is cooked through and tender. Add the ground spices and cook, stirring, for an additional minute.

Carefully mix in the couscous, peach, and almonds and heat through gently, stirring occasionally.

You can omit the almonds if your child
suffers from a nut allergy.

Green Giant Pasta

Serves 4   This is a recipe for fresh green pesto, but the ready-made variety can be used if preferred or if time is short. Pesto is a real favorite with many children and just a spoonful transforms pasta or rice.

9½ oz/275 g dried linguine, spaghetti, or
   tagliatelle

8 new potatoes, halved or quartered if large

2 tsp olive oil

½ cup frozen baby peas

1–2 tbsp pine nuts, toasted in
   a dry skillet

green pesto

2 oz/55 g fresh basil leaves

2 garlic cloves, crushed

generous ¼ cup pine nuts

½ cup olive oil, plus extra
   for covering

4 tbsp freshly grated Parmesan cheese, plus
   extra for serving

salt and pepper

Pesto sauce can be the perfect foil for sneaking in other green vegetables. For example, you could add chopped frozen spinach or broccoli florets. If you don't overdo it, you can just about get away with it!

First **make** the pesto. **Put** the basil, garlic, and pine nuts in a blender or food processor and process until chopped. Gradually **add** the oil and then the cheese and **process** to a coarse purée. **Season** to taste with salt and pepper. **Spoon** the pesto into a jar with a lid. **Pour** over enough oil to cover. **Use** immediately or store in the refrigerator for up to a week.

Cook the pasta in a large pan of boiling water according to the package directions, then **drain**, reserving 2 tablespoons of the cooking water.

Meanwhile, **cook** the potatoes in a pan of boiling water for 10 minutes, or until tender. Drain, then **cut** the potatoes into bite-size cubes.

Heat the oil in a large pan and add 4–6 tablespoons of pesto, and the potatoes and peas. Heat the mixture for a few minutes, then **season** to taste with salt and pepper. **Add** the pasta and the reserved cooking water. Heat through and **mix** in the pine nuts.

Serve sprinkled with Parmesan cheese.

Teriyaki Tuna with Vegetable Noodles

Serves 4   Children are far more inclined to eat fish, particularly the stronger-flavored oily type, if marinated first. Asian flavors always go down well and a spoonful of honey adds a sweet, caramel flavor.

4 tuna steaks, about 4 oz/115 g each,
   cut into strips

marinade

½ cup bottled teriyaki sauce

2 tsp honey

salt and pepper

vegetable noodles

8 oz/225 g dried medium egg noodles

1 tbsp corn or sunflower-seed oil

2 tsp sesame oil

1 carrot, cut into thin strips

2 bok choy, stems and leaves separated and
   finely sliced

1 yellow bell pepper, seeded and cut into
   thin strips

2 garlic cloves, chopped

1 tbsp soy sauce

to serve

2 scallions, diagonally sliced

toasted sesame seeds

Mix the teriyaki sauce, honey, and salt and pepper to taste together in a shallow dish. Add the tuna and turn to coat in the marinade. Cover with plastic wrap and let marinate in the refrigerator for 1 hour, turning the tuna occasionally.

Cook the noodles according to the package directions. Meanwhile, preheat the broiler to high. Line the broiler pan with foil. Remove the tuna from the marinade, reserving the marinade, and arrange in the broiler pan. Spoon over half the marinade and cook under the broiler for 1 minute. Turn over, then spoon over the remaining marinade and cook for an additional minute.

Preheat a wok until hot. Add the oils and swirl around the wok. Stir-fry the carrot, bok choy stems, and yellow bell pepper for 2 minutes. Add the garlic and bok choy and stir-fry for 1 minute. Add the soy sauce and a little water. Drain the noodles and divide between 4 bowls. Top with the stir-fry, tuna, and any cooking juices, and sprinkle with the scallions and sesame seeds.

Fresh Fruit Sticks

Serves 4   Children can help to assemble these colorful, vitamin-rich fruit sticks, but they do need adult supervision if they are very young. The fruit sticks can be broiled or barbecued and are excellent served with a dollop of thick plain yogurt or a good-quality vanilla ice cream. If using wooden skewers, soak them in water for 10 minutes beforehand to prevent them burning.

**choose from a selection of fresh fruit—
pineapples, mangoes, bananas, kiwifruit,
peaches, and oranges are best, cut into
½-inch/1-cm chunks
honey or maple syrup, for brushing**

Preheat the broiler to high and line the broiler pan with foil. Thread the fruit onto skewers and arrange on the broiler rack.

Heat the honey in a small pan until very runny and brush liberally over the fruit using a pastry brush.

Cook the fruit under the broiler, turning frequently, for 5–8 minutes, or until the fruit softens and the honey begins to caramelize.

You can also serve the fruit sticks uncooked, but make sure that the fruit you use is perfectly ripe and juicy.

Banana & Vanilla Malt

Serves 4   This energizing smoothie is wonderfully thick, creamy, and satisfying.

Try adding strawberries, peaches, nectarines, or mango instead of the bananas. For a healthier drink, the ice cream can be omitted and 1¼ cups of the milk replaced with thick plain yogurt.

3 cups milk
2 large bananas, sliced
6 tbsp malt drink powder
4 scoops good-quality vanilla ice cream
ice cubes, to serve

Put the milk, bananas, and malt drink powder in a blender or food processor and **process** until blended and smooth. **Pour** into 4 tall glasses, then **add** a scoop of ice cream to each glass and a few cubes of ice.

Apple & Carrot Juice

Serves 4   This classic juice is a sneaky way of encouraging your child to eat vegetables. The lemon juice enhances the flavor and helps to retain nutrients.

4 large dessert apples, cored and quartered
3 carrots, peeled and trimmed
squeeze of fresh lemon juice

Put the apples and carrots through a juicer, then stir in the lemon juice. Serve immediately—the juice does not keep well.

Double Chocolate Brownies

Makes 16   For an occasional sweeter treat, you could make these tasty brownies. If you use pieces of broken chocolate, be sure to just serve a small piece of brownie. It also makes a great birthday cake.

5¹/₂ oz/150 g semisweet chocolate with a
   minimum of 70 percent cocoa solids
7 tbsp unsalted butter, plus extra
   for greasing
1 tsp vanilla extract
1 cup ground almonds

scant 1 cup superfine sugar
4 eggs, separated
generous ¹/₂ cup chopped raisins or pitted
   dried dates, chopped walnuts, or chocolate,
   broken into small pieces
confectioners' sugar, to decorate (optional)

Preheat the oven to 350°F/180°C. **Grease** an 8-inch/20-cm square cake pan and line the bottom.

Put the chocolate and butter in a heatproof bowl, then set the bowl over a pan of barely simmering water, making sure that the bottom of the bowl doesn't touch the water, and heat, stirring very occasionally, until melted and smooth.

Carefully **remove** from the heat and let cool slightly, then stir in the vanilla extract. **Add** the almonds and superfine sugar, then mix well until combined. Lightly **beat** the egg yolks in a separate bowl, then **stir** into the chocolate mixture, with the dried fruit, walnuts, or pieces of chocolate.

Whisk the egg whites in a large, grease-free bowl until stiff peaks form. Gently **fold** in a large spoonful of the egg whites into the chocolate mixture, then **fold** in the remainder until well incorporated.

Pour into the prepared pan and **bake** in the preheated oven for 25 minutes, or until risen and firm on top but moist and gooey in the center. **Remove** from the oven. Cool in the pan, then **turn out**. Remove the lining paper and cut into 16 pieces. **Dust** with confectioners' sugar to decorate, if using.

Index